Music and Technologies 2

Music and Technologies 2

Editor:

Darius Kučinskas

Assistant Editor:

Georg Kennaway

Cambridge
Scholars
Publishing

Music and Technologies 2

Editor: Darius Kučinskas
Assistant Editor: Georg Kennaway

This book first published 2014

Cambridge Scholars Publishing

Lady Stephenson Library, Newcastle upon Tyne, NE6 2PA, UK

British Library Cataloguing in Publication Data
A catalogue record for this book is available from the British Library

ISBN (10): 1-4438-7074-9
ISBN (13): 978-1-4438-7074-0

TABLE OF CONTENTS

PREFACE

DARIUS KUČINSKAS

Music and Technologies 2 continues research discussions initiated in 2011 with an international conference held at Kaunas University of Technology, Lithuania. Selected papers from this conference were published in 2013 in the book with the same title – *Music and Technologies. Music and Technologies 2* is a collection of articles from the conferences held in 2012 and 2013. The main aim of this book is to continue discussions in the field of music technologies, to involve new themes and to extend ideas in the interdisciplinary music research developed at such important meetings as CIM (Conference on Interdisciplinary Musicology) and ISMIR (International Society for Music Information Retrieval). The book also explores some of the main contemporary ideas in the field of using music technologies in the compositional process, performance practice, music installations, and understanding the role and importance of these technologies in contemporary musical life.

The question of electroacoustics as a separate discipline is discussed in a text by the English researcher James Mooney. Understanding the connections between acoustic and visual media is presented in an article by the American musicologist Paulo C. Chagas. Italian musicologist Franco Fabbri presents an overview of the aesthetic and technological aspects of phonographic, not cinematic, stereo sound from 1958 to date, and the contradictions that happened to stereophonic sound. An Austrian researcher Gregor Widholm discusses some inquiries into technology in music acoustics and performance science. These questions are developed with practical experience presented in the texts of two contemporary composers: Simonetta Sargenti (Italy) and Neringa Žaltauskaitė (Lithuania). The cognition of music structures is analyzed by three researchers from Jävaskylä University. Finally, different aspects of applied technologies in classical music recording, including the distinction between music and noise recording, are explored in articles by the Lithuanian researchers Vytautas Kederys and Antanas Kučinskas.

We anticipate this book will be useful for those music researchers and practitioners who are involved in e-music composition, performance and analysis. Some parts of the book will be relevant for music educators and students. Others can serve as good examples of music analysis and research, applying new interdisciplinary methods and tools. The book is supported with a CD-ROM where audio and video files from the articles are included.

CHAPTER ONE

LES MUSIQUES ÉLECTROACOUSTIQUES: CONSTRUCTION OF A DISCIPLINE

JAMES MOONEY
UNIVERSITY OF LEEDS

For the past three years, I have been studying the work of the English musicologist Hugh Davies. Davies was well-known as a performer, and builder of his own idiosyncratic electronic musical instruments, but in this chapter I will be focusing on his work as a researcher and documenter of electronic music during the 1960s. My hypothesis is that Davies redefined what electronic music *was* during that period, and, that his definition of electronic music still holds true today (at least as far as electronic music in an academic context is concerned). My argument, in essence, is that Hugh Davies constructed the discipline of what is now known as electroacoustic music.

Two questions are as follows. First of all, *how* did Davies go about constructing a discipline of electroacoustic music? To answer that question, I will examine Davies's published and unpublished research work from 1961–1968. Second, to what extent was he successful? Or, to put it another way, to what extent has Davies's definition of electronic music been accepted? To answer this second question, I will examine subsequent published literature and projects from 1968–2012 that have cited or been based on Davies's work, and show how the structure of Davies's model of electronic music is reflected in this subsequent work.

The strategies that Davies used were as follows. First, he mapped the existing territory of electronic music in a number of documents and publications between 1961 and 1964. Then, from 1966–1968, he adjusted and extended the map to meet his own specifications, providing, in effect, a new model—a new vision—of electronic music. Third, while he was doing this he also made sure that he fought off any competition, so as to ensure that it would be *his* map—not someone else's—that would define electronic music in the future.

Davies started to map the territory, first of all, with a brief and sketchy "Survey of Electronic Music and *Musique Concrète*", written while he was still at school (Davies 1961*), then with a discography in which he started to catalogue electronic music on record and tape (started in 1962, published in 1964, supplement in 1966; Davies 1964, 1966), then by writing an extended historical overview for his undergraduate dissertation (Davies 1963*), and then—in an article entitled "New Directions in Music"—by providing a set of hypotheses on future developments (Davies 1963). In these studies, Davies identified a number of different *disciplines*, published *discourses*, and identified *countries* in which relevant activities were taking place. *Musique concrète*—the discipline of music with recorded every-day sounds—was practised in France and discussed in a book by Pierre Schaeffer (Schaeffer 1952); *Elektronische Musik*—music with electronically generated sounds—practised in Germany and documented by Eimert and Stockhausen (1955); and "computer music" in the United States (Illinois), described in a book by Lejaren Hiller and Leonard Isaacson (Hiller 1959).

In the early 1960s, much electronic music activity took place in isolated disciplinary, discursive, and geographic enclaves as just described. What Davies did that was original and innovative was to begin to write about these fragmented disciplines as if they were the constituent parts of single praxis; he began to place the various fragmented discourses into a single historical narrative of electronic music. This process had already started to some extent, as reflected in some of the literature from this period. Two other books mentioned in Davies's research are Prieberg's *Musica ex Machina* (1960) and Judd's *Electronic Music and Musique Concrète* (1961), both of which attempted some degree of generalisation rather than focusing on a single individual discipline. Davies was rather critical of the latter, but described the former as "the most useful book yet issued, [...] unfortunately not yet translated into English" (Davies 1964, 207). My suggestion is that Davies took this process of generalization further than any preceding author had, and in rather different directions.

Davies also began to identify activities in countries less usually associated with the genesis of electronic music, such as Poland and Japan. Davies thought that it was important for countries to retain their national identities, musically speaking, because he felt that the international cross-fertilisation of distinct musical traditions was a potent force of musical innovation (Davies 1963). Because national identity was important for Davies, he tended to classify things by nationality, and we see that reflected in his writings (Davies 1961*, 1963, 1984*).

Having mapped the existing territory, Davies then began to adjust and extend the map to his own specifications, providing in effect a new model of electronic music. He did this by compiling and publishing what was his *magnum opus* of this period—a 330-page volume entitled *Répertoire International des Musiques Électroacoustiques / International Electronic Music Catalog*, started in 1966 and published in 1968 (Davies 1968). In the *Catalog*, Davies attempted to list every single piece of electronic music in existence, anywhere in the world. He also produced appendices in which he attempted to identify all uses of electronic music in Poetry, Jazz, Sculpture, Painting, and a number of other interdisciplinary areas. In other words, he expanded his initial map of electronic music by adding extra disciplines; by documenting the existence of electronic techniques in areas not traditionally associated with art-music composition. The *Catalog* is arranged alphabetically by country, representing a continuation of Davies's tendency to classify by nation, and also ensuring that all countries—including less well-known ones—were represented equally. Within each country, individual studios are listed, and under each studio there is a chronological list of the compositions realised there, including details of the composer, title of the work, the duration, the number of channels, and so on. The composers are all listed in an index at the back of the *Catalog*, so that it is possible to discover all of the works of a particular composer. The lists of electronic music works are classified according to their function: as seen in Table 1-1, the system of classification devised by Davies included works intended for concert performance, or as a sound-track for a theatre performance, or intended for radio broadcast, and a number of other categories. This was another way in which Davies sought to classify electronic music in a way that made it his own: by defining the various categories into which works of electronic music could fall.

When Davies compiled the *Catalog,* he sent a questionnaire to studio managers. In it, he did not ask completely open questions, but rather, he asked about particular things. For example, Davies specifically asked studio managers to provide information on electronic music that was connected with painting or sculpture. He did not ask, for instance, about electronic music works involving dance. If he *had* asked studio managers about electronic music in dance, one wonders, how might the picture painted by the *Catalog* be different? Davies also asked studio managers to classify the electronic music works realised at their studios according to his own predetermined system of functional classifications (see Table 1-1). Studio managers were not allowed to invent their own classifications: they had to pick from one of the options that Davies had prescribed. If Davies had allowed studio managers to specify their own classifications, again, one wonders, how might the emerging picture have been different? The point I'm making here is that Davies, to some extent, shaped the answers he received according to the questions that he asked, and this is one of the ways he designed a model of electronic music to meet his own specifications.

Table 1-1. Functional classifications of "electronic music" used by Davies in the *Catalog*.

Standalone music	**Applied music**	
	Live	**Recorded**
C (tape)	O (opera)	F (film)
C+ (tape & insts.)	B (ballet)	R (radio)
C* (live electr.)	Th (theatre)	TV (television)
(c = concert)	MT (music theatre)	D (disc)
	Sn (sonorisation)	In (interval signal)
		St (study)

While compiling the *Catalog*, Davies made deliberate efforts to fight off the competition. For example, a musicologist based at a university in the United States—Dr Sven Hansell—had produced a document entitled "A Provisional List of Electronic Music Compositions" (Hansell 1966), dated February 1966—several months before Davies had even started work on his *Catalog*. Through quite a long series of letters and correspondence (Davies 1967*), Davies eventually made sure that Hansell would not publish his *Catalog* commercially; a step towards ensuring that his own project would not have any major competition.

Turning now to my second question: to what extent was Davies successful in defining electronic music? To what extent has the model of electronic music built by Davies in the 1960s been accepted? The *Catalog* was published in 1968, and since then, quite a substantial body of literature has cited it. What we find is that the structure of the *Catalog* is quite conspicuously reflected in that body of literature, as shown in Table 1-2. For example, there are a number of studies that focus on the electronic music of a particular nation or geographic area, reflecting the *Catalog*'s alphabetic organisation by country (Farra 2006; Kuluntausta 2008; Zajicek 1995). There are studies that focus on a particular studio, or on a particular composer (Garcia-Karman 2010; Giomi 1995), because those things are quite easy to look for in the *Catalog*. There are also a number of published articles that are based on one or another of the *Catalog*'s appendices; for example, an article on the history of electro-acoustic approaches to sound poetry (Wendt 1985). There are even some published articles that are based upon the "number of tracks" column in the main part of the *Catalog*. Simon Emmerson, for example, makes the observation that the first experiments in multi-channel sound—conducted at the GRM in Paris in the early 1950s—were carried out quite some time before multi-channel tape-music became common. In other words, multi-channel sound was "invented" (if you like) as a live performance activity, and it wasn't until later that it was used in the studio. The data that Emmerson uses to back up that argument are the data that appear in the "number of channels" column in the *Catalog,* which shows that almost all the works at the GRM studio were monophonic up to 1958, some seven years after the live performance experiments in multi-channel sound (Emmerson 2007, 150). Elsewhere, Manning (2006) makes use of the "tracks" column in a similar way.

There are also at least two quite prominent textbooks that use the data contained within the *Catalog* as the basis for making some quite general assertions about the nature of electronic music history. Manning, in *Electronic and Computer Music*, talks about an "exponential growth" in electronic music during the 1960s and uses statistics from the *Catalog* as the proof of that (Manning 2004, 401-02). Similarly, Thom Holmes, in *Electronic and Experimental Music*, notes that the number of electronic music studios worldwide increased dramatically between 1948 and 1966, again using statistics drawn from the *Catalog* to prove this (Holmes 2012, 154).

Table 1-2. Organisational features of the *Catalog* versus bodies of literature citing it.

Organisational features of the *Catalog*	**Bodies of literature citing it**
Organised alphabetically by country	Studies focusing on electronic music of a particular nation / geographic area
Organisation by individual studios	Studies focusing on the output of an individual studio
Composers indexed	Studies focusing on the work of an individual composer
Appendices mapping out different disciplines	Studies looking more closely at those disciplines
Works listed under a number of headings	Studies making use of the information under those headings

Landy, in an article on the musicology of electroacoustic music, even goes so far as to use the *Catalog* as a general pointer to the entire "history of [electroacoustic] music (and its pre-history)" (Landy 1999, 64), on which topic he footnotes the *Catalog*. Such examples illustrate the *Catalog*'s totemic status as a unique record of historical activities in electronic music, to the extent that the *Catalog* is sometimes even used as a symbolic representative of electronic music history itself.

The *Catalog* also continues to play an important role as an inventory. At the time it was compiled, Davies was at pains to point out that it was the first ever attempt to catalogue every piece of electronic music in existence, and that it would never be possible to attempt such a thing again (Davies 1968, v). And, he was right, because even today the *Catalog* is (as far as we know) the closest thing in existence to a complete inventory of electronic music compositions up to the end of 1966—or, at least, a complete list of the compositions that meet Davies's definition.

In the 1990s, the *Catalog* was used as the basis of a new project—*Internationale Dokumentation Elektroakustischer Musik* or 'EMDoku' for short (Hein 1999). That project used the *Catalog* to provide the data for compositions up to the end of 1966, and began the process of adding pieces composed after that date, using the format and system of classifications prescribed by Hugh Davies in the *Catalog*. (Actually, the classification system used in EMDoku is slightly adapted from Davies's, but remains very similar.) The EMDoku database has been identified by the director of the Groupe de Recherches Musicales, Daniel Teruggi, as the closest thing in existence to a complete inventory of all electronic music (Teruggi 2004). This is another example of how Davies's work continues to define electroacoustic music in the present day.

In conclusion, what I have tried to show is that, during the early 1960s Hugh Davies set out to map the territory of electronic music, by writing about it historically as part of a grand tradition, by emphasising activity in different parts of the world, and by producing a discography and thereby starting to index it. Then, with the *Catalog*, he started to extend that map so that it more closely reflected his own particular view of what electronic music should be. In particular, he thought that electronic music should be interdisciplinary—including activities such as sculpture, poetry and painting as well as activities more traditionally associated with the electronic music studio. He thought it should be international; not in the sense of a single, homogeneous, global praxis, but rather, representing all nations as equals, and celebrating their distinct national identities. In turn, we see the structure of the *Catalog* reflected in subsequent literature that cites it, and in subsequent projects that build on its principles and systems of classification. In my view, this demonstrates that the *Catalog* occupies an important position in electroacoustic music history, and is therefore worthy of wider recognition and closer academic attention.

References

(Those marked * are unpublished sources from the Hugh Davies Archive, British Library.)

Davies, Hugh. 1961*. *A Survey of Electronic Music.*
—. 1963. New Directions in Music. *The New University* 12, 8–17.
—. 1963 [JM3]*. *Electronic Music and Musique Concrète: An Historical Survey*. (Oxford).
—. 1964. A Discography of Electronic Music and Musique Concrète. *Recorded Sound: The Journal of the British Institute of Recorded Sound*, 14, 205–224.
—. 1966. A Discography of Electronic Music and Musique Concrète: Supplement. *Recorded Sound: The Journal of the British Institute of Recorded Sound*, 22-23, 69–78.
—. 1967*. Letter to Sven Hansell, undated c. February.
—. 1968. *Répertoire International Des Musiques Electroacoustiques / International Electronic Music Catalog.* Paris & Trumansburg, NY:

Groupe de Recherches Musicales de l'ORTF & Independent Electronic Music Center, Inc.

Eimert, Herbert, and Karlheinz Stockhausen. 1955. *Electronic Music*, *Die Reihe.* New York: Theodore Presser.

Emmerson, Simon. 2007. *Living Electronic Music.* Aldershot: Ashgate Publishing Ltd.

Dal Farra, Ricardo. 2006. Something Lost, Something Hidden, Something Found: Electroacoustic Music by Latin American Composers. *Organised Sound*, 11, 131–142.

García-Karman, Gregorio. 2010. Roberto Gerhard's Tape Collection: The Electronic Music, in *Proceedings of the 1st International Roberto Gerhard Conference: May 27-28th 2010*, 2010, p. 107–122; <http://www.robertogerhard.com/wp-content/uploads/2011/10/15-Karman.pdf> [last accessed 20 May 2013].

Giomi, Francesco. 1995. The Work of Italian Artist Pietro Grossi: From Early Electronic Music to Computer Art. *Leonardo*, 28, 35–39.

Hansell, Sven Hostrup. 1966. *A Provisional List of Electronic Music Compositions*. University of Illinois School of Music, Experimental Music Studio.

—. 1967*. Letters to François Bayle, Henri Chiarucci, Hugh Davies, Robert Moog, and Reynold Weidenaar, 8 February 1967 to 23 May 1968.

Hein, Folkmar. 1999. 'Internationale Dokumentation Elektroakustischer Musik'; <http://www.emdoku.de/> [accessed 18 April 2013].

Hiller, Lejaren. 1959. *Experimental Music : Composition with an Electronic Computer.* Westport, Conn: Greenwood Press.

Holmes, Thom. 2012. *Electronic and Experimental Music: Technology, Music, and Culture*, 4th ed. New York: Routledge.

Judd, Frederick Charles. 1961. *Electronic Music and Musique Concrète.* London: Neville Spearman.

Kuljuntausta, Petri. 2008. *First Wave: A Microhistory of Early Finnish Electronic Music.* Helsinki: Like.

Landy, Leigh. 1999. Reviewing the Musicology of Electroacoustic Music: A Plea for Greater Triangulation, *Organised Sound*, 4, 61–70.

Manning, Peter. 2004. *Electronic and Computer Music.* Oxford: Oxford University Press.

—. 2006. The Significance of Techné in Understanding the Art and Practice of Electroacoustic Composition, *Organised Sound*, 11, 81–90. <doi:10.1017/S1355771806000112>

Ojanen, Mikko. 2012. 'Helsingin yliopiston elektronimusiikkistudion varhaisvaiheet'; <https://helda.helsinki.fi/handle/10138/37412> [last accessed 3 March 2013].

Prieberg, Fred K. 1960. *Musica ex Machina: Über das Verhältnis von Musik und Technik.* Berlin: Ullstein.

Daniel Teruggi, 'Electroacoustic Preservation Projects: How to Move Forward', *Organised Sound*, 9 (2004), 55–62.

Wendt, Larry. 1985. Sound Poetry: I. History of Electro-Acoustic Approaches II. Connections to Advanced Electronic Technologies. *Leonardo*, 18, 11–23 <doi:10.2307/1578088>.

Zajicek, Libor. 1995. The History of Electroacoustic Music in the Czech and Slovak Republics. *Leonardo Music Journal*, 5, 39–48.

CHAPTER TWO

AUDIOVISUAL AND MULTIMEDIA COMPOSITION: UNDERSTANDING THE CONNECTIONS BETWEEN ACOUSTIC AND VISUAL MEDIA

PAULO C. CHAGAS
UNIVERSITY OF CALIFORNIA, RIVERSIDE

The concept of audiovisual and multimedia art is shaped by the dominant role of film and television in our society. The technology of sound and image reproduction that became available in the second half of the 19th century was the foundation of audiovisual and multimedia creativity. However, we see emerging new forms of audiovisual art, which explore manifold connections between sound, music, image, body, movement, space, etc. This process becomes more and more differentiated with the popularization of digital technology and the predominant role of digital networks of mass distribution. This article investigates audiovisual and multimedia composition on the basis of the distinction between *medium* and *form*, which was proposed by Luhmann in the realm of the theory of art as a social system (Luhmann 2000).[1] I will examine these concepts, their historical context and their application to the understanding of the connections between visual and acoustic media. Finally, I will discuss the electronic music video as a genre and present an example of my own audiovisual composition, the work *The Journey* created in 1995 in collaboration with Inge Kamps.

"Medium" and "form" are not understood as structures, but as concepts accounting for operational distinctions made by an observer. "Medium" is defined as a loose coupling of elements, "form" as a tight coupling of elements (cf. Luhmann 2000, 104). The medium consists of elements or of events in the time dimension, but these elements are only loosely connected. Form, by contrast, arises from the "concentration of relations of dependence between elements, i.e., thorough selection from the possibilities offered by a medium" (Luhmann 1990b, 216). The medium is defined by the nature of the loose elements of which it consists, but the medium is only perceived through the form that coordinates its elements. As Luhmann explains: "We do not see the cause of light, the sun, we see things in the light. We do not read letters but with the help of the alphabet, words" (Luhmann 1990b, 216).

The distinction between medium and form can also be understood as a distinction between *chaos* (*entropy*) and *order* (*negentropy*), as used in information theory (Shannon) and cybernetics (Wiener). In *The Human Use of Human Beings*, Wiener expounds a vision of cybernetics as a science that contends against the natural tendency of the universe to deteriorate and lose its distinctiveness, to move "from a state of organization and differentiation in which distinction and forms exist, to a state of chaos and sameness" (Wiener 1954, 12). Cybernetics uses probabilistic and statistical methods to calculate and predict how information comes into being from an indeterminate, chaotic state. When information emerges from chaos, it becomes a fundamental attribute of communication. From mathematics and statistics, cybernetics moves towards a theory of knowledge extending the probabilistic view of the world to the social sphere. In the age of information, the cybernetic study of communication requires an understanding of the mechanisms of control underlying the exchange of information between man and machine and between machines themselves. Although the universe tends to run down, Wiener believes that "there are local enclaves whose direction seems opposed to that of the universe at large in which there is a limited and temporary tendency for organization to increase" (Wiener 1954, 12); and organizing life in these enclaves is the task of the new science of cybernetics.

The idea of a chaotic universe underlying life is expressed also by the distinction between *randomness* (*noise*) and *pattern*. Wiener suggests the metaphor of the organism as being a message through which the organism emerges from a background of randomness to constitute itself as a pattern of organization:

> Organism is opposed to chaos, to disintegration, to death, as message is to noise. To describe an organism, we do not try to specify each molecule in it, and catalogue it bit by bit, but rather to answer certain questions about it which reveal its pattern; a pattern which is more significant and less

probable as the organism becomes, so to speak, more fully an organism. (Wiener 1954, 95)

By focusing on the body, recent humanistic studies have reversed the tendency of cybernetic and computational thinking to treat information as an abstract concept, disconnected from a physical structure. Nowadays, body metaphors frame the discourse on information. In *How We Became Posthuman*, Katherine Hayles reconstructs the distinction between randomness and pattern in the so-called "posthuman" society. In opposition to the computational account of information as a non-material entity, Hayles' vision of the posthuman emphasizes the role of embodiment and materiality in the processes of constituting meaning: information includes both the technical meaning of information and the perception that information is a code carried by embodied entities. Hayles proposes a representation of meaning in the form of a semiotic square with two axes: the main axis is the distinction between *presence* and *absence*; the secondary axis is the distinction between *randomness* and *pattern*. Two diagonals that connect these two axes trigger a dynamics of signification. The diagonal connecting presence and pattern conveys *replication*; the diagonal connecting absence and randomness signals *disruption*. The interplay between presence and absence shapes materiality; the interplay between randomness and pattern gives rise to information (cf. Hayles 1999, 247-251; see Figure 2-1).

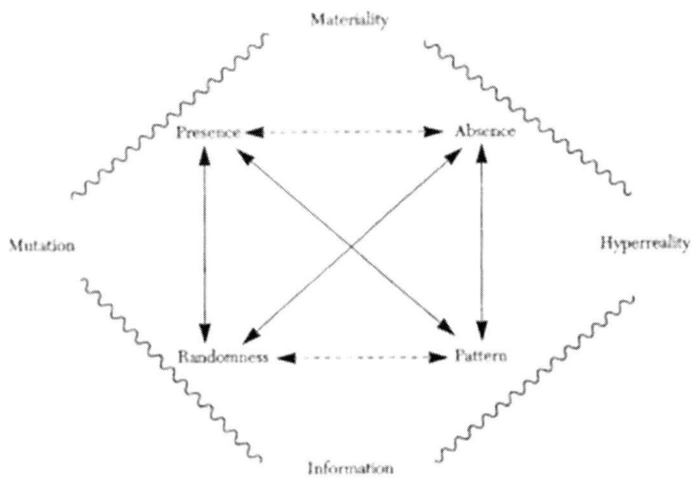

Fig. 2-1: The interplay between randomness and pattern (Hayles 1999, 249).

Hayles envisions the posthuman as a more sophisticated way to approach the world of new technologies in which the human is seen not as an autonomous self but as part of a chaotic and unpredictable world. Instead of assuming an attitude of panic—as cybernetics does by assigning to itself the task of reversing the natural process of entropy—Hayles suggests that we have to accept the "posthuman"; it means that we should abdicate from taking control of the world and try to "maximize human potential in a world that is in essence chaotic and unpredictable" (Hayles 1999, 291).

What is the use of the distinction between medium and form for analyzing artistic forms? As Luhmann points out, art depends on primary media such as acoustics and optics. Sound objects and events are shaped in the acoustic medium; visual objects and events are shaped in the optical medium (Luhmann 1990b, 218). Furthermore, art also needs a higher medium in order to communicate. The most general medium of art is the so-called medium of "meaning" [*Sinn*].[2] Meaning is processed through the distinction between actuality and potentiality. The form thus selectively reduces the combinatory possibilities of the medium. The actualization results from selective processing that restrains and limits the connecting possibilities. For example, any sound can be combined with any other in a temporal flow, but in a piece of music there must be some constraints in selecting which sound follows the previous one. Each new sound actualizes the potential of musical work. The result is that the distinction that creates meaning is itself a form that allows subsequent distinctions in time; i.e., "meaning is a form that creates forms in order to assume forms" (Luhmann 2000, 108). In short: the form updates and renews the medium by coupling and uncoupling it. The form processes a selection of distinctions that actualizes its potential.

This recursive character of the distinction between medium and form is what allows the reproduction of meaning. Every distinction between medium and form creates "a form with two sides, one of which—the side of the form—contains itself" (Luhmann 2000, 104). In other words: "meaning is also a form that on both sides contains a copy of itself in itself" (Luhmann 1998, 50). Each new operation that creates meaning is a re-entry of the distinction medium and form in one of its sides.[3] The successive operations through which a medium is transformed into a form, then into a medium, then into a form, and so on, generate a recursive network of distinctions, a feedback-loop mechanism that ultimately drives and controls the system itself. This leads thus to an evolutionary conception of meaning, which applies also to art.

The distinction between medium and form is based on the view that society is a self-referential and closed system, an "autopoeitic" system that produces and reproduces communication. Art is a sub-system of society sharing the same characteristics of the society in terms of autonomy and operational closure. Art communicates through works of art, which can be considered as "compact communication or as a program from innumerable communications about the work of art" (Luhmann 1990c, 194). Art can only function as communication for those who can distinguish the difference between medium and form and communicate about it. Art articulates the difference between medium and form by making available new possibilities of form building. For example, medieval music created the medium of modality for distinguishing melodic forms, the medium of polyphony for harmonic forms. Furthermore, music created the medium of tonality, the medium of atonality, the medium of electroacoustics, and so on.

Luhmann argues that artistic evolution can be described "as the increase in the capacity for dissolution and recombination, as the development of ever new media-for-forms" (Luhmann 1990b, 221). Modern art has appropriated media such as the human body, society, technology, and even art itself—for example, the works of art that are staged as paradox (Duchamp and Cage). An artwork comes into being through an operation that transforms an unmarked space into a marked space and creates a boundary by crossing that boundary. The determination of one side makes also the other side accessible. The work of art cannot reject the world; it invites us to discover further distinctions that can be made by observing the work of art itself and what is left outside. The work of art thus stimulates the crossing of its own boundaries. This double function of art is what permits us, for example, to keep performing and listening to the music of the past. Any new interpretation of the music by Bach, Mozart, Beethoven, etc. allows us to gain new insights into both the marked and the unmarked space of these works. The aesthetic experience accomplishes the paradox of making visible what is invisible. The music of the past becomes itself a medium for new distinctions of forms.

The focus on "medium"—and on related concepts such as "mediality", "medialization", "medial thinking", etc.—dominates studies on digital art and music, particularly in the German-speaking countries. There is a tendency to interpret sound as a "media object" and to categorize aesthetic issues according to the media structures and channels. This is evident, for instance, when emerging genres such as "sound art", "radio art", and "soundscape" are elucidated as media-specific forms; or when one claims that the far-reaching "medialization of sound" impacts the "compositional forms, structures and aesthetics concepts until it finally questions our traditional understanding of music" (Harenberg 2012, 7-8).[4] Media studies and communication studies offer very different theories on the history and the structures of media. But overall they deliver a vision of media shaped by the reality of the mass media and media technologies. The difficulty of such a consideration appears when one asks whether there is a special medium for that which we today call audiovisual art. The main reference is of course the film, in which the image is at the forefront and the music plays mostly a secondary role. The relation between image and sound in film is thus an asymmetric one.[5] The cinema is the symbol for the dominance of technical images in our society, but we see emerging other audiovisual forms with a more differentiated relationship between sound and image: from experimental film to video, from musical composition to sound installation, from concert to multimedia performance (not forgetting the video game, which has evolved into a powerful medium using new technologies and unfolding an unpredictable, ambiguous potential of creativity).[6] Media studies focused on information tend to assign a privileged role to digital technology in the constitution of the "audiovisual" and the "multimedia". Digital technology is considered a new form that brings about the convergence of channels and the integration of formats through multimodal coding. From this point of view, multimedia is defined as "a multimodal aggregation of digital media" (Hartmann 2008, 8). Friedrich Kittler, who remains maybe the most influential German media theorist, shapes the discourse on digital technology with a radical pessimistic tone:

> Before the end, something is coming to an end. The general digitization of channels and information erases the differences among individual media. Sound and image, voice and text are reduced to surface effects, known to consumers as interface. Sense and the senses turn into eyewash. Their media-produced glamour will survive for an interim as a by-product of strategic programs. Inside the computers themselves everything becomes a number: quantity without image, sound, or voice. And once optical fiber networks turn formerly distinct data flows into a standardized series of digitized numbers, any medium can be translated into any other. With numbers, everything goes. Modulation, transformation, synchronization; delay, storage, transposition; scrambling, scanning, mapping a total media link on a digital base will erase the very concept of medium. Instead of

> wiring people and technologies, absolute knowledge will run as an endless loop. (Kittler 1999, 1)

From the perspective of critical and phenomenological studies of digital media, "sound" and "vision" are crucial references. The reproduction technology introduced in the 19th century created new possibilities for the arrangement of medium/form relationships associated with the primary media of "acoustics" and "optics". They reconstructed our experiences of "hearing" and "seeing". Digital technology represents a further step in the transformation of the audio and visual experience. Recent accounts of digital technology focus on models of embodied and extended cognition in the construction of meaning, affecting also our understanding of sound and vision. In *The Auditory Past*, Sterne argues that the "boundary between sound and not-sound is based on the understood possibilities of the faculty of hearing" which is grounded in our bodily practices (Sterne 2003, 12). The practices of sound reproduction, as Sterne claims, have to be understood in relation to other bodily practices. In *Philosophy for New Media*, Hansen analyzes how digital visual media engage the body in the process of creating meaning. With digital media, the body has the function of filtering information and providing an affective supplement. Hansen sees a "fundamental shift in aesthetic experience from a model dominated by the perception of a self-sufficient object to one focused on the intensities of embodied affectivity" (Hansen 2004, 12-13).

These preliminary considerations should have made clear that the audiovisual and multimedia represent a complex field of investigation. It is necessary to develop a comprehensive account of the relation between "sound" and "image" beyond the conventional forms of the film in order to bring up the connections between music, sound and visual art. It is also necessary to critically review the discourses on digital media, pointing out the broad spectrum of possibilities of audiovisual and multimedia composition, in terms of both convergence and differentiation of media and forms.

The Electronic Music Video as Audiovisual Genre: *The Journey*

The popularization of digital technology has accelerated the convergence of sound and image in artistic creation. Audio and video recording, editing, and processing can be accomplished with the computer using similar techniques, sometimes integrated in the same virtual environment. Both the digital audio workstation (DAW) and the digital video workstation, for instance, support this integrative approach by providing the artist with a set of hardware and software devices, tools, and plug-ins. Moreover, the technology available to individuals can practically match the quality standards of today's professional audio and video production.

Let's examine the music video clip as a new genre of popular audiovisual composition. The music video clip emerged as a filmed version of a song performance and became a mass consumption product in the 1980s thanks to MTV. From the media of film and television, the music video clip has migrated to the internet, whereby its aesthetics have evolved from being a provider of visual illustration for a song into a medium for shaping and sharing individual and collective behaviors, attitudes, identities and political views. Launched in 2005, the website YouTube has taken the "aura" out of the production of the music video clip, converting it into a global art object. Anyone can make a music video clip, upload it onto the internet, and eventually be discovered or acknowledged as an artist. YouTube is the medium that accomplishes the worldwide banalization of the music video clip; it redraws the boundaries between the system of art and the system of mass communication while unfolding a new kind of creativity, which conveys the ambivalence of information and communication technologies. (Global networking creates new forms of freedom but also sets new boundaries for freedom. It opens up new possibilities for individual and collective exchange and at the same time develops new strategies for monitoring and controlling these exchanges, such as the mechanisms that are embedded in certain websites, such as Google). The music video clip is the emblematic archetype of a form that emerges from the convergence of film and music and transforms itself into a medium for shaping new audiovisual forms in the digital society.

Let's now turn our attention to the music video that arose out of the tradition of "serious" electronic music. The intermedia form, coupling electronic sounds with image projection, enjoys growing interest and is developing into a sub-genre of electroacoustic music. The music can be "heard" and "seen" at the same time. The audiovisual merge seems to have the potential to make the music more accessible to a broader audience. But here, one has to raise the following question: Does the multimedia intensify the sensory experience and make it thus more attractive, or does it simply provide a distraction that reinforces the patterns of entertainment and diversion in everyday life? Whatever the answer may be, embedding the music into an audiovisual form provides the listener with an immersive experience that is functionally linked to the situation of the movie theater: the music is projected into the room through loudspeakers, the sound surrounds the bodies, while the image projected onto a screen—usually located in front of the audience—focuses the audience's attention on an illuminated surface. The electroacoustic music video relating sound, image, and space is primarily an immersive experience that can be also integrated with other forms, such as the concert with live music performance (vocal, instrumental, and/or electroacoustic music); the performance with dance and acting; the installation; and so on. Traditionally, the audiovisual art is structurally coupled with the space both as physical and social medium. The immersive experience relates physical presence to social presence. By contrast, watching an electroacoustic music video on a computer, on the internet, or on a mobile device is mainly an individual experience, in which the embodied experience is dispersed along a spectrum of possibilities emerging from the interaction with the technological environment.

In the following, to illustrate the genre "electronic music video", I will introduce an example of my own work, *The Journey*, a collaboration with the German visual artist Inge Kamps. I became acquainted with Inge Kamps in 1995 when we both participated in the "Babel" group, a project by artists from Cologne for developing collaborative work. Hans-Ulrich Humpert, composer and director of the electronic studio at the Musikhochschule in Cologne (he was my teacher), had invited me there, and he likewise collaborated with Inge Kamps at a later date. The electronic music video *The Journey* was created in 1995 as the first result of my collaboration with Inge Kamps and premiered in the event "Best of Babel" at the Musikhochschule in Cologne. Two other music videos followed—*Einblick* (1995) and *Zeit-Wände II* (1997)—as well as the music video installation *Zeit-Wände VII* (2003).

The electronic music of *The Journey* (length: 9:16) was composed for a multimedia work *Global Village—Hidden Pathways*, performed in 1993 in Bonn, Germany. It was developed in collaboration with the BEC (Bonn Research Center of Computer Media) and the American visual artist Doris Villa. The electronic music was integrated into an interactive holographic environment and the live performance of a singer. For *The Journey*, Inge Kamps created a new videography in 1995 on the base of the electronic music, trying to creating a synchronism between sound and image. The visual composition uses as source material footage of four motifs—water, earth, oscillograph, and mind-machine—as abstract textures and patterns in synchrony with the music. The aesthetics of *The Journey* emphasizes the correlation of auditory and visual perception: the two layers of experience are meant to stand over against each other as equals and at the same time create a close structural connection, by which an intermedial unity results. With the synchronism of auditory and visual perception, the electronic music video pursues the concept of a time-space synesthesia. From my point of view, *The Journey* is a very successful example of the exploration of synesthetic perception in audiovisual art (http://soundof cities.commagazine/moviesby/thejourney.html).

The composition received an award from the Internationaler Videokunstpreis SWF/ZKM in 1997.

Notes

[1] The medium/form distinction reproduces the system/environment distinction that serves as the basis for Luhmann's theory of social systems (cf. Luhmann 1984). Luhmann revised and reformulated his theory again and again. A further discussion of the medium/form distinction can be found in Luhmann's later *Die Gesellschaft der Gesellschaft* (1997, 190–202). The many essays that Luhmann dedicated to art and literature over the space of more than 20 years reflect also the continual development of his theory (cf. Luhmann 2008). For English translations cf. Luhmann 1995 (translation of Luhmann 1984); 1990a (a collection of essays); and 2013 (a series of lectures).

[2] "Meaning is the medium that allows the selective production of all social and psychic forms. [...] In relation to Edmund Husserl's phenomenology, meaning is for Luhmann the premise of every processing of experience: meaning points in the surplus of references to further possibilities of experience in each individual experience". (cf. Baraldi, Corsi, and Esposito 1997, 170).

[3] George Spencer Brown introduced this idea of form as distinction in his book *Laws of Form*, which is a constant reference in Luhmann's theory. For the concept of "re-entry", see Spencer Brown (1969, 56).

[4] For an account of media from a German perspective see: Kittler (1999), Hartmann (2000), and Kloock and Spahr (1997).

[5] Michel Chion's book *Audio-Vision* (Chion 1994) offers a comprehensive account focused on cinema of the relations between sound and image.

[6] Manovich proposes a theory of new media based on the differences between new and old media. He claims that cinema was the first media to make use of the principles that shape new digital media (cf. Manovich 2000, 49-51).

References

Baraldi, Claudio, Giancarlo Corsi, and Elena Esposito. 1997. *GLU: Glossar zu Niklas Luhmanns Theorie sozialer Systeme*. Frankfurt am Main: Suhrkamp.

Chion, Michael. 1994. *Audio-Vision*. Translated by Claudia Gorbman. New York: Columbia University Press.

Hansen, Mark. 2004. *New Philosophy for New Media*. Cambridge, MA: The MIT Press.

Harenberg, Michael. 2012. *Virtuelle Instrumente im akustischen Cyberspace: Zur musikalischen Ästhetik des digitalen Zeitalters*. Bielefeld: Transkript.

Hartmann, Frank. 2000. *Medienphilosophie*. Vienna: WUB.

—. 2008. *Multimedia*. Vienna: Facultas.

Hayles, Katherine. 1999. *How We Became Posthuman: Virtual Bodies in Cybernetics, Literature, and Informatics*. Chicago: University of Chicago Press.

Kittler, Friedrich. 1999. *Gramophone, Film, Typewriter*. Translated by Geoffrey Winthrop-Young and Michael Wutz. Stanford, CA: Stanford University Press.

Kloock, Daniela, and Angela Spahr, eds. 1997. *Medientheorien: Eine Einführung*. Munich: Wilhelm Fink.

Luhmann, Niklas, 1984. *Soziale Systeme: Grundriss einer allgemeinen Theorie*. Frankfurt am Main: Suhrkamp.

—. 1990a. *Essays on Self-Reference*. New York: Columbia University Press.

—. 1990b. “The Medium of Art.” In Luhmann, 1990a, 215–26.

—. 1990c. “The Work of Art and the Self-Reproduction of Art.” In Luhmann 1990a, 191–213.

—. 1995. *Social Systems*. Translated by John Bednarz, Jr., with Dirk Baecker. Stanford, CA: Stanford University Press. [English translation of Luhmann 1984]

—. 1997. *Die Kunst der Gesellschaft*. Frankfurt am Main: Suhrkamp.

—. 1998. *Die Gesellschaft der Gesellschaft*. Frankfurt am Main: Suhrkamp

—. 2000. *Art as Social System*. Translated by Eva M. Knodt. Stanford, CA: Stanford University Press. [English translation of Luhmann 1997]

—. 2008. *Schriften zu Kunst und Literatur*. Edited by Niel Werber. Frankfurt am Main: Suhrkamp.

—. 2013. *Introduction to Systems Theory*. Edited by Dirk Baecker. Translated by Peter Gilgen. Cambridge: Polity Press.

Manovich, Lev. 2000. *The Language of New Media*. Cambridge, MA: MIT Press.
Spencer-Brown, George. 1969. *Laws of Form*. London: George Allen and Unwin.
Sterne, Jonathan. 2005. *The Audible Past*. Durham; London: Duke University Press.
Wiener, Norbert. 1954. *The Human Use of Human Beings: Cybernetics and Society*, 2nd ed. Garden City, NY: Doubleday.

Chapter Three

Whatever Happened to Stereophonic Sound?

Franco Fabbri
University of Turin

Stereophonic sound, and its mass dissemination since the late 1950s, has been commented on by audio engineers and music critics, but quite scarcely by musicologists, with the notable exception of Allan Moore's conceptualization of the *soundbox* (Moore 1992; Dockwray and Moore 2010; Moore 2012, 29-44), and scholars in the recent field of 'the Art of Record Production' (Lacasse 2005; Moylan 2007 and 2009). Stereophonic sound has often been considered as a 'trick' by record companies and music scholars alike, and even thorough analyses of recordings and/or components in the audio chain have given just passing attention to stereo, as if nothing had changed in high-fidelity since the age of mono. Even if digital technologies have largely enhanced the potential of sound spatialization, stereo remains to date as something that is 'given', and music commentators seem to be interested in it only when writing (nostalgically or ironically, or both) about the exaggerated stereo effects of mid- to late-1960s pop records. A cultural and musicological assessment of stereo still remains to be done.

Nostalgic hi-fi fans complain that 'new' stereo systems do not seem to be designed for 'real listening', with their small plastic speakers and their far too powerful subwoofers. And kids do not seem to worry when they share their iPod's earphones, listening to just half (the left or the right channel only) of the audio signal from their mp3 files. Maybe the advocates of hi-fi and stereo in the late 1950s and 1960s wouldn't have thought that more than fifty years later the 'wonderful world of stereo' (as it was often described then) would become so dull: but, as a matter of fact, the whole story of audio in the past half century seems more to be a search for compromise, for the 'right fidelity' in a definite listening context, than a quest for excellence. This paper will offer an overview of the aesthetic and technological aspects of phonographic (not cinematic) stereo sound from 1958 to date, and their contradictions.

Fidelity: to what?

When we connect our PC or smartphone to a Wi-Fi network, we don't bother about the meaning of that 'Fi'. Official documents released by the Wi-Fi Alliance suggest that the name is an acronym, standing for 'Wireless Fidelity', but one of the Alliance's founders declared that the name (used for the first time in 1999) is meaningless. Its sound and graphic appearance are shaped on other well-known acronyms, like Hi-Fi (High Fidelity), or Sci-Fi (Science Fiction). Sci-Fi, in turn, was first used in 1954 (by Forrest J. Ackerman, a science fiction collector), based on the then current popularity of Hi-Fi. The term 'High Fidelity' was invented, according to one source, 'by Harold A. Hartley, an engineer working at English Electric in about 1926 as a description of the improved radios and electric gramophones' (Dearling and Dearling 1984, 86). According to the same source, 'the first widespread use of the words "high fidelity" occurred around 1934, used by radio stations in America, in particular WQXR in New York' (*ibid.*). Anyway, the so-called 'Golden Age of High Fidelity' (based on industrial advances that took place in the 1930s and 1940s) spans from the 1950s to the mid-1960s; audiophiles define the late 1960s (the years when transistors were substituted for tubes in Hi-Fi amplifiers) as 'A Near-Death Experience for High Fidelity', followed by 'The Rise from the Ashes' (the 1970s), by a decade (the 1980s) when 'The Fashion-Magazine Gatekeepers Take Over', and by another decade of innovation, the 1990s (Olson 2005). Definitely, at the end of the 1990s the Hi-Fi concept was still popular enough to be used as a reference for the inventors of Wi-Fi (see Figure 3-1 and Figure 3-2).

The concept of fidelity itself is at the base of the early development of audio recording and reproduction: Nipper (belonging to a species known for its faithfulness) recognizes his master's voice, so HMV's iconic logo effectively combines two qualities—the dog's faithfulness and the phonograph's fidelity—into one strong image (see Figure 3-3).

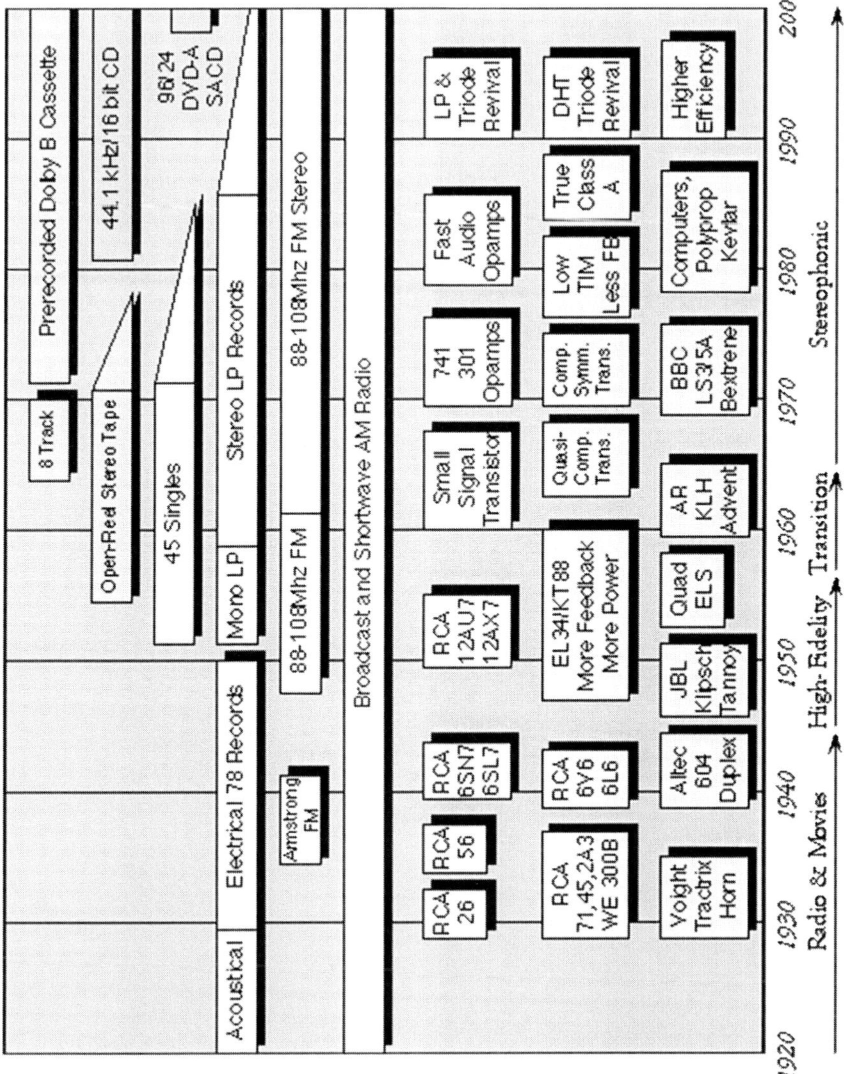

Fig. 3-1: Milestones in Audio (Olson 2005)

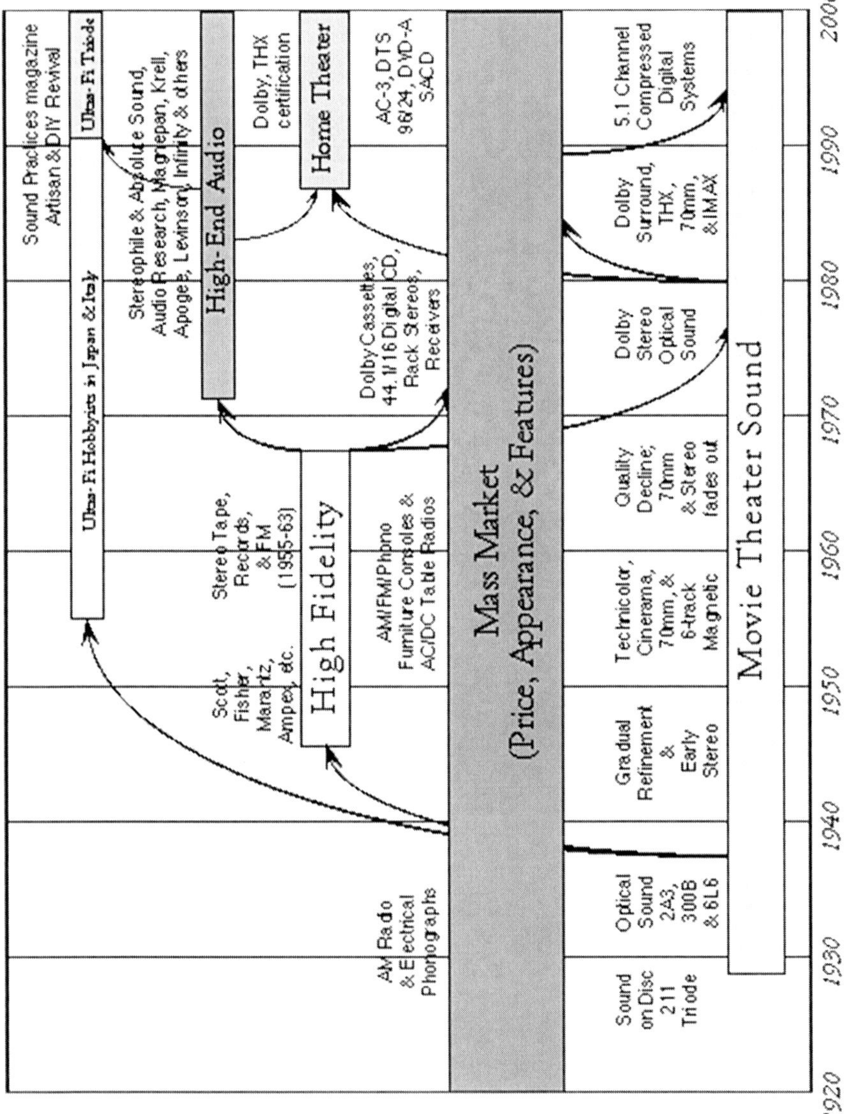

Fig. 3-2: Technology and the Growth of Audio Markets, from Olson 2005

Fig. 3-3: Nipper (original painting by Francis Barraud, 1898)

Although the high fidelity concept emerged in the age of electric recording, and has since then been associated with technological advances and with a growing obsession for measures such as frequency range, signal-to-noise ratio, third harmonic distortion, and the like, fidelity was already a key concept in the mechanical age, before any measuring technology for audio signals was introduced. Still in the age of mechanical recording, Edison's Tone Tests were aimed at convincing prospective buyers that they wouldn't be able to distinguish the sound of a recording from a live source (a singer or an instrumentalist performing the same material at the same time): both the record player and the performers were hidden behind curtains, and attendees were asked to tell if the live source was active or not. The trick was that the record player was never stopped, so the noise produced by the scratching of the needle on the record's surface was always present. It can be said that the test itself was based on the acceptance of an audile technique (using Jonathan Sterne's term) consisting in the 'unconscious' cancellation of the system's inherent noise, a technique that any listener to phonograms like shellac or vinyl records or cassettes should remember very well.

For decades, high fidelity has been primarily associated with the idea of recreating the sound of a concert hall in the listener's living room. The coincidence of the Golden Age of High Fidelity with the advent of stereophonic sound (first, in 1955-56, with open-reel two-track tape recorders, and after 1957 with Westrex stereophonic records) is a proof of the importance of the listener's sensation (even on the basis of an imperfect illusionary technology) in comparison with any technical measurement (see CD-ROM Movie files 01 and 02).

Early demo records offered live recordings, often commentated by a radio-styled presenter, with the aim to direct the listener's attention to the spatial 'realism' of the recorded sound (see Figure 3-4).

Fig. 3-4: A Journey into Stereo Sound, 1958

Listening to stereophonic records

As used to be well known until recently, the stereophonic effect is properly created if the listener is located at the vertex of an equilateral triangle, with the system's two loudspeakers located at the two other vertices. The bulk and expensiveness of early stereophonic systems fitted with the so-called 'average listener's' living room: Hi-Fi was for upper middle-class families, and the recorded repertoire was aligned with their tastes: classical music, jazz, crooners, refined orchestral 'light music' (Mantovani and the like); no rock 'n' roll. It may be the effect of chance, but the decline of rock 'n' roll in the late 1950s in the USA, and the time 'when the music died' ('American Pie'), coincide exactly with the rise of stereophonic records. Pop and rock records, at that time, were aimed at different listening contexts: juke-boxes, FM radios, small monophonic record players used by teenagers in dorms or in their own rooms, where collective listening sessions with peers often took place (see Figure 3-5 and Figure 3-6).

It is known that until the second half of 1963, the Beatles recorded on two tracks, and their stereo releases (especially made for albums to be released in the US) simply presented the vocal track on one channel and the basic instrumental track on the other; but it wasn't just because of such technical limits that George Martin wasn't in favour of stereo mixes: he thought that the band's audience wasn't interested in stereo, and most probably wouldn't own a stereophonic player (see Figure 3-7).

Fig. 3-5: Teenager listening to her records.

Multitracking was more common in the USA, but most pop records were anyway mixed down to mono. A notable exception is represented by the 'techno' bands of the early Sixties, which were later dubbed 'surf bands', like the Ventures in the USA and the Shadows in Britain: especially, American bands were supported by middle-class students living on the West Coast, who loved the technological sound and look of electric guitars and amplifiers (Hoskyns 2003, 58). So the Ventures' and

Fig. 3-6: College students listening to records together.

Fig. 3-7: Sound engineer Norman Smith, Ringo Starr and George Harrison listening in one of Abbey Road's control rooms (presumably in 1964).

Shadows' *albums*, since 1960-1961, were mixed in stereo. The release of stereo *singles* was delayed by the fact that until FM stereo stations overcame AM mono stations in the late 1970s, radio broadcasts were largely in mono, and record engineers as well as record company managers feared that phase cancellation could damage their products' sound.

The advent of transistors in professional and Hi-Fi audio equipment design brought many changes: while, according to audiophiles, it worsened the quality of amplifiers (Olson 2005), it also made Hi-Fi equipment cheaper and more compact (making car stereos possible), and was at the basis of very fast improvements in professional audio equipment, allowing the development of multitrack recorders and multichannel mixing desks, which in turn enabled producers and musicians to use the recording studio as a compositional tool. Only seven years separate 'I Want to Hold Your Hand' (the first Beatles' recording on four-track) from Pink Floyd's *Atom Heart Mother*, or from Miles Davis *Bitches' Brew*, two in a multitude of albums where the idea of 'a concert hall in your living room' can't be applied, not only because they are based on studio recordings, but mainly because—due to overdubbing and editing—an actual live performance of the material presented in those records never took place anywhere.

The experience of a stereophonic recording became more and more widespread, overcoming earlier limits:

> Stereo was for the high-tech freaks. Mono was for the masses. Not only did stereo albums cost a dollar more, but they often came with a warning on the record jacket that they should only be played on stereophonic equipment. The concern was that the heavy needles often used on cheap mono record players would ruin the stereo albums. Even in America, where stereo record players were making inroads, most albums were pressed in a ratio of 90% mono, 10% stereo up until 1966, when the switch to stereo began. (Spizer, n.d.)

In 1967 stereo headphones were made available for the first time to the general public, and many young people spent hours and hours during that summer listening to the Beatles' *Sgt. Pepper's*, as witnessed by Paul Simon in an interview for the movie *The Rutles: All You Need is Cash* (Idle and Weis, 1978)[1] (see CD-ROM Movie file 03).

Only one year earlier, 8 Track Stereo had been made available for car usage, and by the end of the decade car radios mounted stereo cassette (Philips) players (see CD-ROM Movie file 04).

Although the loudspeaker spatial configuration in a car is far from the ideal triangle, and the engine's and aerodynamic noises make the overall signal-to-noise ratio problematic for Hi-Fi listening, nonetheless the combination of proximity and loudness makes the car listening experience similar to that allowed by headphones. The car became (and in my opinion still is, although inexplicably undervalued by most scholars and critics) one of the main places for the individual and collective listening of recorded music, second only to listening at home or in colleges.

Recording studios soon adopted alternative speaker systems to allow engineers, producers and musicians to listen to the actual 'end result' of their work: near field monitors, whose perceived sound is independent of the control room's acoustics and helps to simulate the typical sound of domestic 'stereos' and shelf loudspeakers, and car stereo speakers.

Far from trying to re-create the conditions of a live event in a concert hall, musicians, producers and engineers listened to their recordings to check if the result corresponded to their intentions, their artistic and/or commercial ambitions, or simply their liking. Over a short period, between the early 1960s and the early 1970s, the allocation of signal sources to the stereophonic panorama in popular music recordings changed from the rudimentary and extreme positions in early stereo mixes to the sophisticated soundscapes of progressive rock albums.

Even some professionals today believe that extreme positions and movements of sources across the panorama in early stereo mixes were just meant to shock listeners, in a well-orchestrated manoeuvre by consumer electronics firms aimed at selling more stereo equipment. Of course, marketing reasons cannot be excluded, although it may be more historically appropriate to say that record companies were responding to consumers' demands. As a matter of fact, that 'stereo aesthetics' was obliged by the scarcity of independent channels on mixing consoles (it took two channels to place a source into an intermediate position, or have it moving, while a single channel could be easily placed full centre, or to the extreme left, or right).[2] As the number of channels increased, and pan-pots became available on each, engineers, producers, and artists felt free to use any position in the panorama. After 1969-70, in an increasing number of productions, the elements of the drum kit were distributed in the stereo panorama. The positioning of sources became a key factor in the preparation of a final mix, implying strategic decisions on the positioning of the listener him/herself: should the listener be placed at a distance (say, right in front of the 'stage'), or within the band or orchestra? Would the listener imagine being involved in the performance (being 'one of them') or just attending? Such decisions were (and still are) of fundamental aesthetic importance, not only for popular music recordings: just think of the recordings of concerts for piano and orchestra, where (often) the piano keyboard is extended over the entire panorama (suggesting that the listener is placed just on the pianists' stool), while the orchestra too occupies the same position (an 'impossible space', as the piano in a concert hall is placed parallel to the stage, and so the pianist—and the imaginary listener sitting with him/her—would hear the violins behind, cellos and double basses in front, winds and percussion on the left, and the (silent) audience on the right: but no classical recordings are made like this).

Stereo mixes and multitrack recording added a new dimension to the high-fidelity debate: is the spatial configuration of the original music event (which?) a primary element of the 'reality' that must be reproduced?

Recording isn't a medium: it's an artefact. It has been so forever, in spite of any ideology of transparency. But the mass diffusion of Hi-Fi in the late 1960s and 1970s brought a new concept: that of the fidelity (high fidelity) *to the recorded master*. And the recorded master became the paradigm, even for live performances. During the same time period mentioned above, PA systems evolved from the primitive configurations of early Beatles' performances (where the audience's screams frequently covered any sound produced on stage, monitors didn't exist, and performers had to stay close, often singing in the same microphone, just to be able to listen to one another) to the spaceship looking PAs (Sci-Fi, as well as Hi-Fi) of Pink Floyd in 1969-70 (see Figure 3-8).

In 1967 the idea of a rock concert was still disconcerting (pun unintended) for musicologist and critic Hans Keller, interviewing Pink Floyd for BBC;[3] by the early 1970s thousands of young people attended, lying down silently on the ground of sports arenas or open-air festivals, performances by groups like Pink Floyd, or Genesis, or others, often based on the enlarged dynamic range and stereophonic effects made available by big Hi-Fi PA systems: performances that were aimed at recreating in those real places the imaginary soundscapes originally conceived for headphones,

Fig: 3-8: A photograph for the cover of Pink Floyd's *Ummagumma* (discarded)

students' rooms, or cars. It was the original concept of high fidelity, just reversed.

Popular music was, in the 1960s and 1970s, one of the main interests for youth in Western industrialized countries, for many concurring reasons: it was among the most easily accessible art forms that could be practised, compared to others that required expensive equipment and complex organization (like cinema) or long professional training (like classical music); it was supported by big industry and media, unlike theatre or visual arts; it didn't compete with other consumption goods, a stereo set being probably the most advanced piece of technology one could buy; it could act as a metaphor for social and political change, and as an entry point to 'other' cultures. As Mick Jagger stated in 'Street Fighting Man' (1968): 'Well, then what can a poor boy do / except to sing for a rock n roll band.' In short, music was important; which does not mean, however, that it deserved the same kind of exclusive attention required by advocates of classical music. It could be listened to while doing other things, like smoking, driving, making love (Pink Floyd's *Dark Side of the Moon* has long been credited for being the most used album during such practice). But it was listened to, over long stretches of time. Pink Floyd's guitarist and composer David Gilmour commented, talking about that famous album:

> Attention spans have changed. The idea of going around to somebody's flat or house and sitting around in a comfy room and having a really good Hi-Fi system and listening to a whole album all the way through, then chatting for a few minutes, then maybe putting another album on … does that happen today? (Rolling Stone, 2011).

There is no contradiction: as international popular music in the 1970s 'exploded' into a multitude of competing genres, scenes and functions, a similar diversification took place in playback apparatuses and listening modes: cassette desks (which entered the Hi-Fi market, thanks to the adoption of Dolby noise reduction), ghetto blasters, sound systems, and discotheque PAs. In a burst of confidence based on the phenomenal rise in stereo equipment sales, the audio industry ventured into one of the most catastrophic projects in its history: quadrophony. Competing standards, high prices and unsatisfactory technical results affected the products, while it became clear that many users of stereo equipment did not place loudspeakers correctly, never listened to recordings sitting in the canonical vertex, and used music in their homes for background listening or as a form of decoration. *Musique d'ameublement*, in Satie's terms, as commented by Brian Eno in the sleeve notes for albums like his *Discreet Music* (1975):

> … I put on the record. Having laid down, I realized that the amplifier was set at an extremely low level, and that one channel of the stereo had failed completely. Since I hadn't the energy to get up and improve matters, the record played on almost inaudibly. This presented what was for me a new way of hearing music—as part of the ambience of the environment just as the colour of the light and the sound of the rain were part of that ambience. It is for this reason that I suggest listening to the piece at comparatively low levels, even to the extent that it frequently falls below the threshold of audibility.

Or *Ambient #4 On Land* (1982):

> I regard this music as environmental: to be experienced from the inside. Accordingly, I considered releasing a quadrophonic version of it: an idea I abandoned upon realizing that very few people (myself included) own quadrophonic systems.
>
> However, I have for some years been using a three-way speaker system that is both simple to install and inexpensive [...]. I arrived at this system by experiment and I don't really know why it works. What seems to happen is that the third speaker reproduces any sound which is not common to both sides of the stereo—i.e. everything that is not located centrally in the stereo image—and I assume that this is because the common information is put out of phase with itself and cancels out.

While in the Golden Age of Stereo, and even later for audio enthusiasts, do-it-yourself was a way to aim at perfection in sound reproduction, at the end of the 1970s and in the early 1980s it became a way to contradict and manipulate industrial standards, and to oppose the ideology of high fidelity itself. In the same years, Sony launched the Walkman.

Mobile listening

The Walkman was, to some extent, an answer to the desire of freedom by listeners obliged to sit in front of a couple of loudspeakers (or, with quadrophony, at the very centre of a square), or to stay close to the stereo system, with headphones plugged into it. The name of the product, and images related to it, suggest the idea of 'walking', and seem to imply an outdoor environment: but it could simply mean that one could 'walk away' from the 'stereo' and from the awkward postures that it sometimes implied (see Figure 3-9).

Fig. 3-9: Listening with headphones before the Walkman.

It also had the effect of obliging users to listen through headphones (earlier) or earphones (later): it made headphone listening a mass phenomenon, and favoured private, individual listening with respect to collective listening. And, in an age of technological advances, it was an immensely successful product based on the downgrading of existing technical possibilities: a cassette player that could not make recordings without connectors to plug it into a stereo preamplifier, a small pleasurable object whose design was more important than its audio specifications. Was it Hi-Fi?

An answer cannot be given only in terms of measurements. It can be said that the copy on a chrome dioxide cassette of a newly bought album, made with a 'good' cassette deck from a 'good' record player, played on a 'good' Walkman and listened to through a 'good' pair of headphones, could offer a better listening experience than that of a commercial cassette recording of the same material, listened to on an average Hi-Fi system, especially if one considers that the former could be listened to anywhere, also in environmental conditions masking possible defects (like tape hiss) in the recording. Mobility was, it goes without saying, the key to the Walkman's success, but I would argue that the Walkman's place in media history is also due to its—so to speak—'relativistic' attitude towards fidelity. Up to that point, and with the possible exception of other mobile systems like car stereos, fidelity and Hi-Fi had been based on absolute values: the sound in a concert hall, the closest similarity of recorded sound to live voices or instruments, technical measurements approaching ideal specifications, the standardized geometry and acoustics of the listening space. The Walkman was the first step in another direction: that of the best fidelity for a specific listening function, mode and/or environment.

When Sony released the Walkman, Sony's engineers were already working on the CD, which benefited from the disaster of quadrophony, prompting Sony and Philips to agree on a common standard rather than competing with different systems. But the CD's project was based on the old 'absolutist' ideology of Hi-Fi: it was, to many respects, its final accomplishment. It must be noted that for almost a decade after the introduction of the product in 1982-3, no effective mobile CD player was produced: still at the beginning of the 1990s, CDs in car stereos couldn't be used whenever the road's surface wasn't completely smooth, and CD portable players (the name of the Sony product was Discman) were bulky, heavy, and suffered from any occasional bump: you couldn't really walk, with an early CD Walkman. The problem was solved only in 1993, when a buffer memory was added to mobile CD players, allowing them to compensate for interruptions due to the laser losing its place. Record industry commentators seem to forget that up until the mid-1990s, consumers (even those who did not own a CD player, but who had friends that owned one) used to listen on Walkman personal stereos and car stereos cassettes recorded by copying commercial CDs, and those cassettes were of course of higher audio quality than commercial cassettes, and also commercial vinyl records. Although the signal-to-noise ratio of a Dolby cassette is inferior to that of a CD, and the crosstalk is bigger, such parameters are better than those of vinyl records that until few years earlier were considered to be at the top of high fidelity. The culture of home taping (originated by the boom of Dolby tape desks in the 1970s) was stimulated largely by the lack of adequate mobile listening systems for CDs. Nonetheless, the record industry, faithful to the old high fidelity standards, was more worried by the appearance of the DAT (Digital Audio Tape) recorder, fearing that consumers could make bit-by-bit copies at 44.1 kHz of the industry's precious digital masters. At a time, in the mid-1980s, when recording studios were investing millions of dollars to purchase multitrack digital recorders and to pursue the perfect sound advertised by the record industry, CBS proposed an implementation of the so-called copycode, based on a circuit (to be included in all DAT recorders) that would stop the recording function when detecting a 'hole' in the frequency range of all commercial CDs. Studio owners should purchase very expensive new digital equipment, and then erase an entire, albeit thin, frequency range from recordings in order to make them copy-protected. When Sony bought CBS, putting the copycode project to an end, they applauded.

Alternative mobile systems were launched even before Discman personal stereos became usable. The DCC (Digital Compact Cassette), launched by Philips in 1992, was a complete failure. Sony's MiniDisc, also launched in 1992, enjoyed moderate success, especially as a portable recorder. Both were based on compressed audio formats, respectively Precision Adaptive Sub-band Coding (MPEG-1 Audio Layer I) and Adaptive Transform Acoustic Coding (ATRAC). Although audiophiles scorned them, for not conforming to the highest audio standards, they sounded (for the average user) better than analogue cassettes and vinyl records. For a niche of consumers, the MiniDisc was an introduction to compressed digital formats, and discussions about any audible difference between non-compressed and compressed digital audio started then, about three years before the mp3 format's final specifications were issued.

Conclusions: liquid fidelity

The advent of downloading and mp3 players could be seen by advocates of Hi-Fi as the final demise of the concept. And it is true that Hi-Fi per se isn't popular anymore: there is still a niche of audiophiles who buy extremely expensive 'high end' or 'esoteric' audio systems, but 'Hi-Fi' isn't used even for selling audio equipment in shopping malls or department stores. And equipment that used to be considered Hi-Fi in the 1970s (like Dolby cassette desks or record players) is now very difficult to find. It is also true that many music listeners behave as if they weren't at all interested in the audio quality of the music they are listening to: couples that share one earphone each, for example, or kids playing ringtones at high volume with their mobile phones. Adam Gopnik recently wrote in *The New Yorker*:

> My own teen-age kids, as obsessed with music as I was, have an entirely different way of listening. They ignore the glowing-tube amp and classy articulate speakers in our living room; they bounce instead to tinny earbuds, and often spend hours listening to Taylor Swift or Radiohead on the still more tinny speakers of their computers. Sound quality seems secondary to some other thing they take from music. Though both are far better musicians than I ever was, singing and playing guitar and piano, they have a more limited conception of larger forms, of the record's two sides, of the symphony's three or four parts, of the swell and structure of a cantata. It isn't a question of classical tastes against pop; it's a question of small forms heard in motion against large forms heard with solemn intent. *Sgt. Pepper's* baffles them as much as Beethoven's *Ninth*. They *snatch* at music as we snatched at movies, filling our heads with plural images (Gopnik 2013, 32).

And when I suggest to my students to sit in the middle of the classroom, in order to listen to stereo effects, they seem not to understand and obey reluctantly. Not to mention the level of the equipment I find in classrooms in Italian universities and conservatories (and, I must say, also in some other European countries), which demonstrates clearly how sensitive to sound and music are upper education institutions. It is also true that record producers in the past years have overcharged new and re-released masters with extreme compression, in order to make them sound louder in noisy environments when listened to with poor earphones (the so-called 'loudness war', see Vickers 2010).

But I consider it as an unfair judgement when I hear someone saying that we live in an age of low fidelity. The term received considerable impulse both by the late 1970s sound aesthetic of punk and experimental music, and by Murray Schafer's writings on modern soundscapes. Yes, urban soundscapes are Lo-Fi (though they seem to be less and less so, at least in some parts of the world), and high-end audio equipment like PCs and Macs with sophisticated sound processing software can be used to produce music with a Lo-Fi feel in it. But, in general, it can be said that more people than ever now listen to an unprecedented quantity of music with an average quality that largely surpasses that of preceding decades. It seems to me that listeners are adapting to a 'Just-Right-Fi' concept, a degree of audio quality that fits with the environmental conditions, modes of listening and music functions. And it must be noted that lossy compressed audio formats such as mp3 are based on the same effect and principle—masking—that lets the degree of audio quality of a system depend on the sonic conditions of the environment. If the iPod can be seen as a radical development of the Walkman concept, then 'Just-Right-Fi' is the development of the relativistic attitude towards fidelity established by the Walkman's designers, under popular demand.

Notes

[1] It is well known, however, that *Sgt. Pepper's* was first mixed in mono, while the stereo version was made later without the attendance of the Beatles.
[2] It must be added that extreme pannings from the early 1960s weren't perceived as so extreme by listeners at that time, as the considerable crosstalk of vinyl stereophonic records helped diminish the effect.
[3] http://www.youtube.com/watch?v=a2vc7XA5M7Y. In the interview, Syd Barrett and Roger Waters talk about the group's efforts to give concerts where the audience listens to the music primarily, compared to gigs in ballrooms with their noisy environment. Responding to one of the interviewer's questions, Pink Floyd musicians confirm they have done already a couple of such concerts, and that they went well.

Bibliography

Dearling, Robert J. and Celia Dearling. 1984. *The Guinness Book of Recorded Sound*. London: Guinness Superlatives Ltd.
Gopnik, Adam. 2013. Music To Your Ears. The quest for 3-D recording and other mysteries of sound. *The New Yorker*, January 28, 2013: 32-39.
Dockwray, Ruth, and Allan F. Moore. 2010. Configuring the sound-box 1965–1972. *Popular Music* 29/02: 181-197.
Hoskyns, Barney. 2003. *Waiting For The Sun. Strange Days, Weird Scenes and the Sound of Los Angeles*. London: Bloomsbury.
Hosokawa, Shuhei. 1984. The Walkman Effect. *Popular Music* 4: 165-180.
Lacasse, Serge. 2005. Persona, emotions and technology: the phonographic staging of the popular music voice. *The Proceedings of the 2005 Art of Record Production Conference*.
Moore, Allan. 1992. The Textures of Rock. In Rossana Dalmonte and Mario Baroni (eds.). *Secondo Convegno Europeo di Analisi Musicale*. Trento: Università degli Studi di Trento: 241-244.
—. 2012. *Song Means: Analysing and Interpreting Recorded Popular Song*. Farnham: Ashgate.

Moylan, William. 2007. *Understanding and Crafting the Mix: the art of recording*, second edition. Boston: Focal Press.
—. 2009. Considering Space in Music. *Journal on the Art of Record Production* 4. http://arpjournal.com/1379/
Olson, Lynn. 1996. *The Soul of Sound*. Oregon: Nutshell High Fidelity.
—. 2005. *A Tiny History of High Fidelity*. http://www.nutshellhifi.com/library/tinyhistory1.html (Adapted from Olson 1996).
Spizer, Bruce. N.d. http://abbeyrd.best.vwh.net/allyouneedisfacts.html [last accessed 10 October 2013].
Vickers, Earl. 2010. The Loudness War: Background, Speculation and Recommendations. *AES 129th Convention*, San Francisco, CA, USA, 2010 November 4-7.

CHAPTER FOUR

TECHNOLOGY IN MUSIC ACOUSTICS AND PERFORMANCE SCIENCE

GREGOR WIDHOLM
INSTITUTE OF MUSIC ACOUSTICS (WIENER KLANGSTIL)
UNIVERSITY OF MUSIC AND PERFORMING ARTS VIENNA

Music Acoustics, if defined as a comprehensive ''Science of Music'', consequently must include ''Playing Music'' and therefore covers a wide range of various phenomena to be analyzed and investigated. In particular, the fact that the player and the instrument form a control loop and interfere with each other requires on the one hand, physical and mathematical methods, and on the other, human physiology, psychology and brain science in order to understand the mechanisms of interaction (see Fig. 1). Consequently the target audience for the results differs: it varies from instrument makers, professional musicians, musicologists and neuroscientists to music teachers and music therapists, etc.

Although some basic findings were already made in ancient Greece (Pythagoras et al.), and the discoveries of the scientists of mediaeval times like Galileo Galilei, Marin Mersenne and Ernst Chladni, up to the famous scientists of the 19th century like Hermann von Helmholtz and Alfonso Giacomo Corti, enormously improved our understanding of the function of musical instruments and the perception of music, there still was a significant lack of knowledge – maybe caused by the traditional distinct separation of science and the arts in the 19th and early 20th century.

Additionally, the differences between the technical language and terminology used by acousticians and musicians traditionally prohibited a fruitful communication between scientists and artists. Consequently, the scientists did not understand the musicians, who created their own language to describe highly complex and partly tricky phenomena by one simple term and vice versa. A typical answer of an acoustician of the 20th century on the description of a phenomenon by a musician concerning, for example, the behavior of the musical instrument in a special situation, was: 'What you tell me is due to physical reasons not possible!'

On the other hand acousticians mostly used over-simplified models of musical instruments because they could not handle the enormous amount of data or, as they lacked the experience of professional musicians, were not even able to realize all the parameters involved. Thus, many facts thought until now to be uncontroversial in the music acousticians' community, had to be revised over the last ten years.

The turnaround took place in the 80s and 90s of the last century and was caused by two trends:

First of all, more and more people had a university degree in music and in physics, engineering or humanities. This enabled them to understand both worlds: science and the arts. Their practical experience as professional musicians helped them to take all relevant parameters into consideration and to avoid an oversimplification of the object of research. In Europe, by and by, new centres developed where scientists exclusively worked in the field of Music Acoustics. The first groups were established around Johan Sundberg at the KTH in Stockholm, Jürgen Meyer at the TU Braunschweig (this group unfortunately was closed down 2003), two in Prague (VUZORT and one at the Music University) and a group strongly related to instrument making companies in Hradec Kralove (Czech Republic) as well as in Klingenthal (former DDR); groups in France included IRCAM in Paris, CNRS in Marseille, and one at the University of Lyon; a group was established around Murray Campbell at the University of Edinburgh (Scotland); and the Institute of Music Acoustics 'Wiener Klangstil' at the University of Music and Performing Arts Vienna was founded in 1980. In Portugal, Spain, Italy, the UK and Norway, various scientists working in Music Acoustics could be found, but not embedded in a separate Institute. This development in Europe is unique, because elsewhere (e.g. USA, Asia and Australia) Music Acoustics Research was (and still is) represented by so-called 'Lone Wolves' like Arthur Benade, Carol M. Hutchins and Tom Rossing from the USA, or Joe Wolfe and Neville Fletcher from Australia.

Secondly, the rapid increase of computing power in the years following the turn of the millennium finally allowed researchers to work with complex models and led for the first time to results effectively matching the reality.

Acoustics of Musical Instruments

Musical instruments are objects which act according to physical rules, but each of the quality parameters defined by the musicians contains several physical parameters with a different weighting. Additionally the control loop between the player and the instrument generates nonlinear effects.

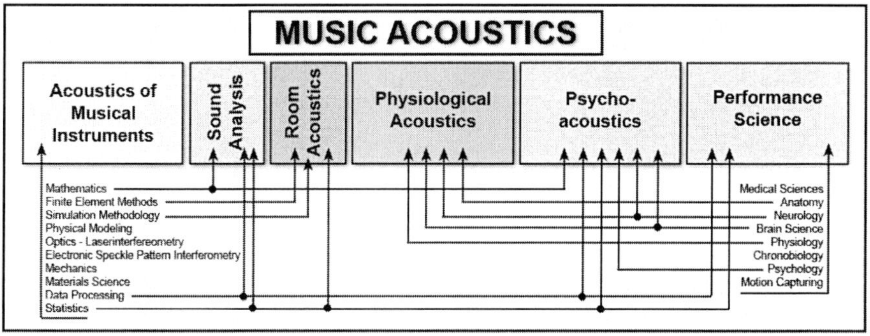

Fig. 4-1: Sub-discipline of Music Acoustics with involved fields of science and their methods.

The auditory quality of an instrument is defined by only one parameter: the sound color, specifically timbre which, of course, is in fact a mixture of the properties of the instrument, the artistic intention of the player and his ability to modify the sound offered by the instrument. For the player, however, the quality of an instrument is defined by several parameters like 'Response', 'Playability' (easy speaking or stiff), 'Intonation', 'Modulation Capability', 'Dynamic Range', the offered basic sound color, etc.

Brass Wind Instruments

At first glance, it seems to be simple: we have a more or less cylindrical and/or conical tube with a closed end at the mouthpiece and an open end at the bell. The principles of function have been well known since the early 20th century: The human lips open and close like a valve (e.g. 440 times per second for an a^1) and push overpressure pulses into the mouthpiece. These pulses form a sound wave with many harmonics and travel down inside the tube of the instrument toward the bell. At the bell 90-94% of the energy is reflected, travels back to the mouthpiece and forms a ‘standing wave’ with the original sound wave. The rest is radiated into the room and represents the sound of the instrument. This works only if the time span of the opening and closing of the lips exactly matches (or is an integer part of) the time required by the sound wave for its round trip from the mouthpiece to the bell and back. Therefore the basic properties and the parameter ‘Intonation’ and to some extent the parameter ‘Response’ can be quantified by an input impedance measurement inside the mouthpiece in the plane of the lips where the standing wave always forms a pressure antinode (Widholm 1995). With such an input impedance measurement (first done in the 1950s), one receives within a few seconds nearly all acoustical properties of the instrument and information on approximately 90% of its musical quality. Figure 4-2 shows the input impedance curves of a good quality (upper curve) and an extremely bad quality (lower curve) French Horn.

At frequencies where the curve forms a peak, a note can be played. As the measurement system – in contrary to the excitation signal of the player which contains a lot of harmonics – works with a sinusoidal excitation signal (chirp), the calculation of the intonation offered by the instrument is valid only for sinusoidal signals. To get practice-oriented results, the calculation must be done by a convolution integral, a so-called ‘weighted sum function’. Figure 4-3 shows an intonation plot for a mid-quality trumpet.

By a transformation of the data from the frequency into the time domain (Inverse FFT and Hilbert transformation), an ‘acoustic radar’ can be simulated and helps us to look inside the instrument and to detect defects (see Figure 4-4).

If the sizes of the instrument (shape of the bore) are known, simulations can save the instrument maker the use of the ‘trial and error’ method for improvements (see Figure 4-5 and Figure 4-6). Transmission line models like that of Mapes Riordan (Mapes Riordan 1993), or spherical and multimodal models (Kausel et al. 1999) have proved their worth.

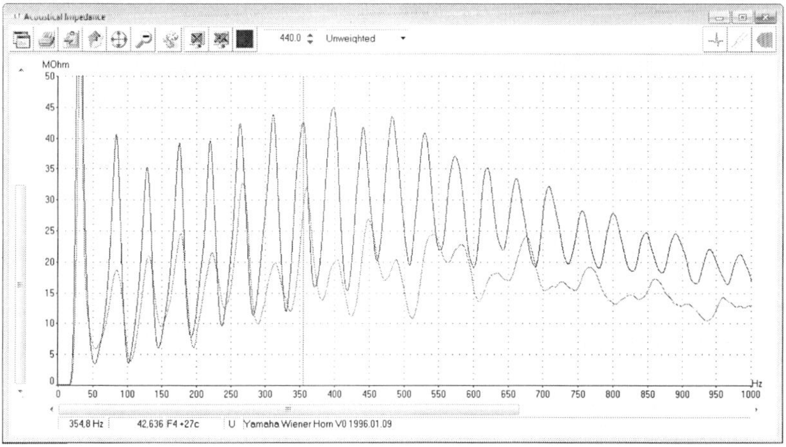

Fig. 4-2: Input impedance of a good quality (upper curve) and an inferior (lower curve) French Horn, measured with BIAS.

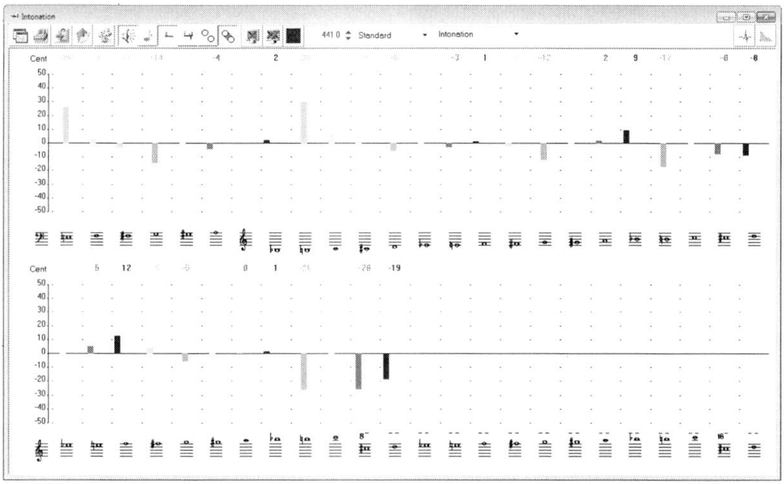

Fig. 4-3: Intonation analysis of a trumpet in Bb based on the measured input impedance. The chart shows the deviation of each playable note from the equally tempered scale in cent. Colors indicate the used fingering (valve combination).

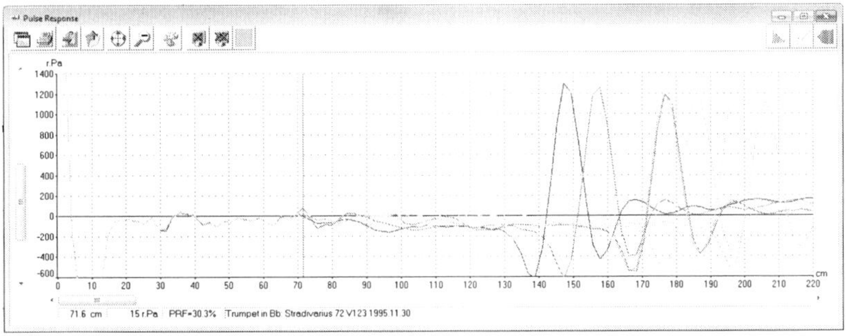

Fig. 4-4: Pulse response of the trumpet of Fig. 4-3. The peaks (right) indicate the end of the bell (blue: open instrument, red: first valve pressed, and so on). The red cursor marks a constriction caused by the first valve at 76.1 cm.

$$a_{11} = \frac{x_1}{x_0}\left[\cosh(\Gamma L) - \left(\frac{1}{\Gamma L}\right)\sinh(\Gamma L)\right]$$

$$a_{12} = \frac{x_0}{x_1} Z_c \sinh(\Gamma L)$$

$$a_{21} = \left[\left(\frac{x_1}{x_0} - \left(\frac{1}{\Gamma x_0}\right)^2\right)\sinh(\Gamma L) + \left(\frac{\Gamma L}{(\Gamma x_0)^2}\right)\cosh(\Gamma L)\right]$$

$$a_{22} = \frac{x_0}{x_1}\left[\cosh(\Gamma L) - \left(\frac{1}{\Gamma x_0}\right)\sinh(\Gamma L)\right]$$

Fig. 4-5: Input impedance of a matrix element.

$$Z_L = \frac{\rho c}{\pi R_a^2}\left(\frac{(k R_a)^2}{4} + i0.6133(k R_a)\right)$$

Fig. 4-6: End resistance at the bell.

Intensive research in this area led in 1999 to the world's first 'Optimiser' software package for brass instruments (Kausel 2001) which allows the input of targets in terms of instrument makers (see Figure 4-7 and Figure 4-8). After the measurement of an existing instrument, the player specifies his wishes in terms of musicians and the optimizer software tells the instrument maker which parts he has to modify to get the desired improvements. Last but not least, the Optimizer can be used to 'clone' instruments or to create new instruments from scratch.

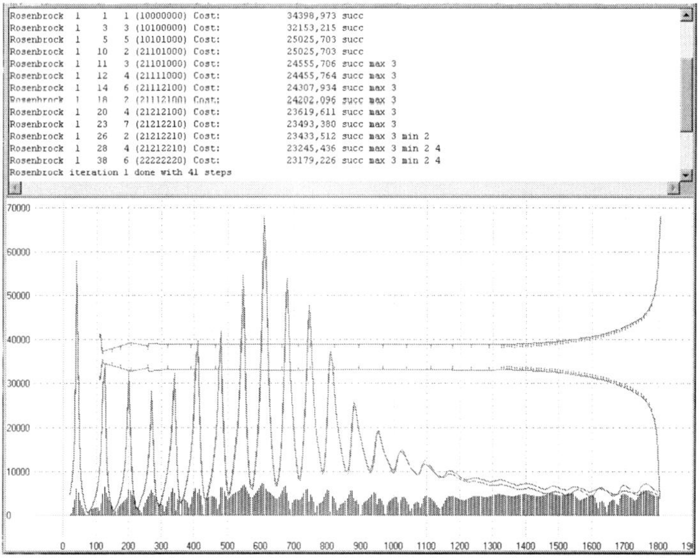

Fig. 4-7: Screenshot of the 'Optimizer' during work. Upper part: Cost factors of the various parameters; lower part: plot of the shape, target impedance and weights for each frequency of the target impedance.

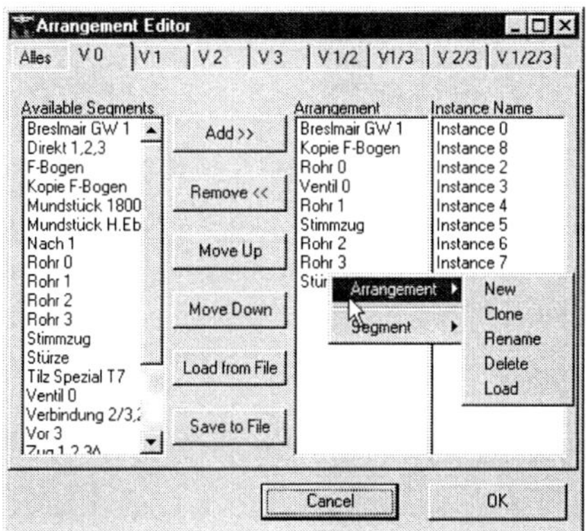

Fig. 4-8: Screenshot of the 'Optimizer'. The arrangement editor allows the combination of various parts to get a complete instrument.

A never-ending controversial topic between acousticians and musicians is the fact that brass players have fixed ideas about the influence of the wall material (alloy) on the timbre and response of an instrument whereas acousticians tend to summarize their point of view by a sentence attributed to Richard Smith, a former trumpet virtuoso and now a well-known instrument maker in York, UK: 'It's all in the bore'. The fact is that the pitch of a played note is defined by the length and shape of the tube. The response (how easy it is to produce the desired note) is mainly defined by the shape of the tube, the mouthpiece and the damping caused by the wall thickness. The timbre depends on the properties of the lips, the damping caused by the wall thickness and the texture of the inner surface. To clear up this subject, it is necessary to take a closer look at brass instruments. Recent research supposes that it has to do not only with one vibrating system (standing wave, air column inside the tube), but with three independent vibrating systems: the air column, the wall of the tube and the instrument as a whole (see Figure 4-9 and Figure 4-10). The vibration of the wall at the pressure antinodes is a parasitic vibration and can cause damping effects on the air column under particular circumstances (Kausel et al. 2010).

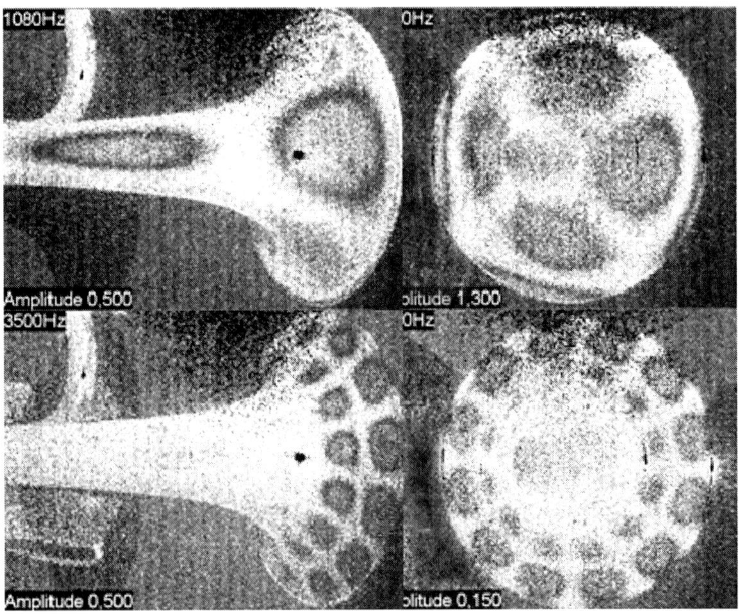

Fig. 4-9: Vibration of a trumpet bell at 1080 and 3500 Hz (ESPI).

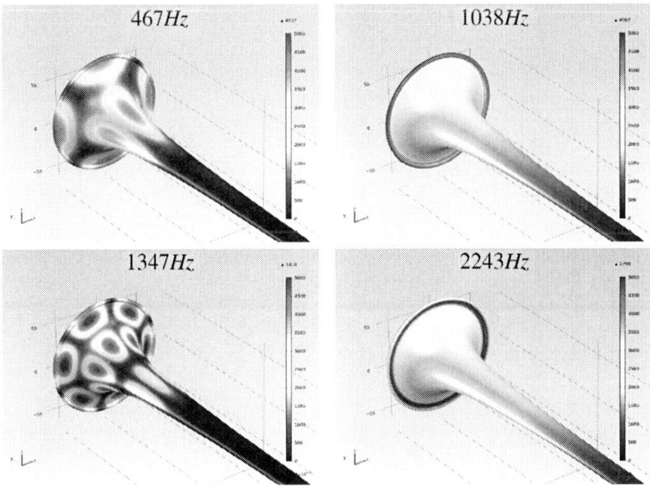

Fig. 4-10: Simulation of trumpet bell vibration. Left: radial modes; right: axial modes including longitudinal vibration.

As braces provide a fixed stiff connection between two parts of the tube, they can inhibit wall vibration if positioned at a pressure antinode. All these effects on the musical quality of brasses are the object of recent research work (Chatziioannou et al. 2012). The third vibrating system (see Figure 4-11) takes the instrument as a combination of various levers and also includes longitudinal/axial vibration caused and transferred to the instrument by the lips and teeth of the player.

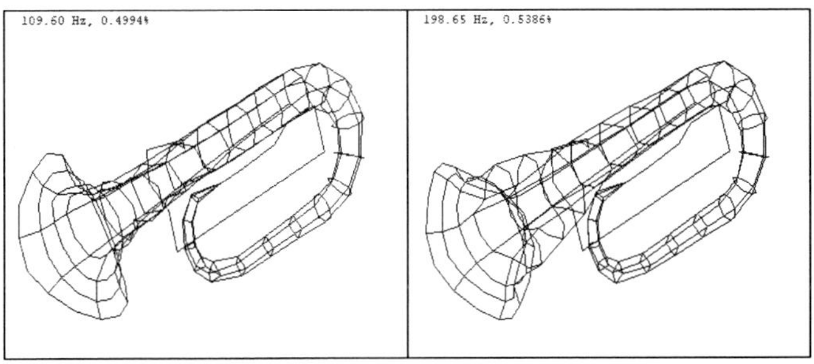

Fig. 4-11: Third vibrating system: longitudinal/axial vibration.

Woodwind Instruments

The crucial factors in the case of woodwind instruments are the excitation mechanism and, to some extent, the properties of the tone holes. Arthur H. Benade's contributions in the 70s and 80s (Benade 1969, 1977, 1983) set the basis for today's research. Special attention has recently been paid to the nature of the air jet of flutes/recorders and the behavior of single and double reeds (Chatziioannou et al. 2012, Kühnelt 2003). Simulations with 3-dimensional fluid-dynamic models using, for example, the Lattice Boltzmann Method give new insights into the aero dynamic phenomena of the air jet and brought up interesting results on losses due to vortex shedding and the influence of the edge shape and the mouth cavity on the sound.

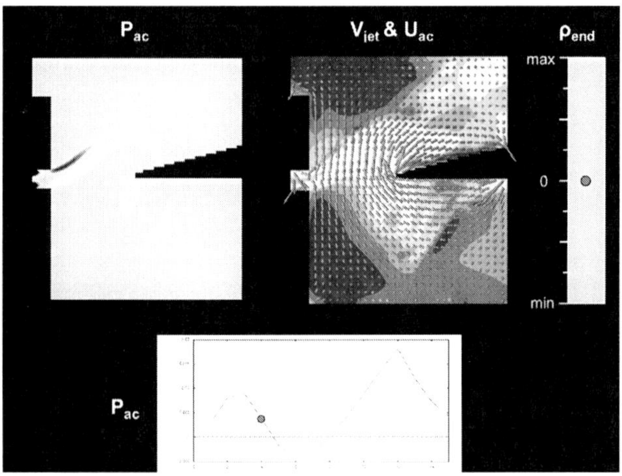

Fig. 4-12: Vortex sound power in a transverse flute.

Similar efforts can be observed in the investigation of the sound generation of single or double reed instruments. In these cases the problem is the anisotropic structure of the reeds. Various research teams have investigated the behavior and the suitability of reeds depending on the parameters density, humidity, stiffness, structure and shape (Dalmont et al. 2003, Guillemain 2004, Hofmann et al. 2012).

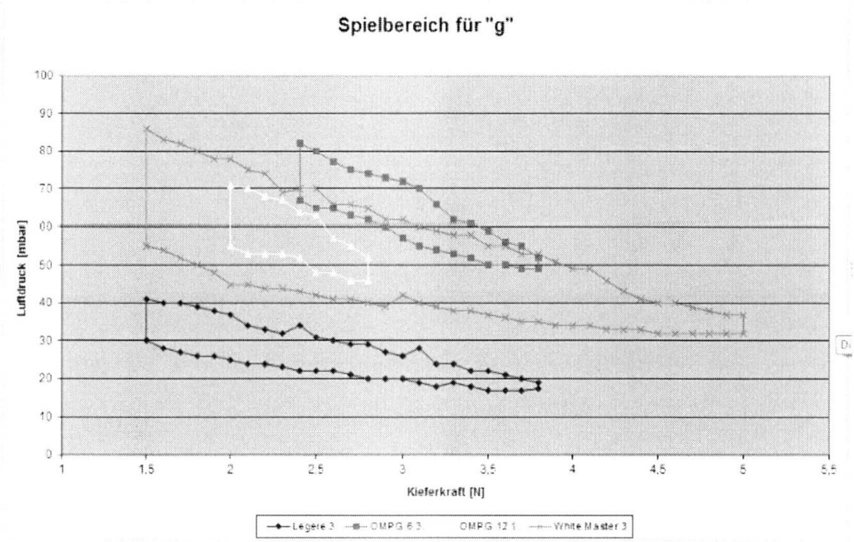

Fig. 4-13: Operating range of Arundo Donax and plastic reeds.

Stringed Instruments

Musically-inclined scientists have often been fascinated by the famous Old Italian violins and have tried to unlock their reputed secrets. Felix Savart (1791-1841) disassembled such violins and investigated the vibration modes of top plates and back plates with the method of his friend E. Chladni. His findings about the relationship between the main modes of the top and back were interesting but not sufficient enough to explain the outstanding quality. Luthiers carried on with the 'trial and error' method. A big step forward was made by Heinrich Dünnwald in the late 1960s by his Transferfunction method. Based only on the measured transfer function, he clearly could differentiate between Old Italian, luthier-made and industrially produced violins (see Figure 4-14).

Almost the same information can be obtained by an admittance measurement where the instrument gets excited by a short impulse at one edge of the head of the bridge. The measurement sensor is mounted at the opposite edge of the bridge (see Figure 4-15 and Figure 4-16).

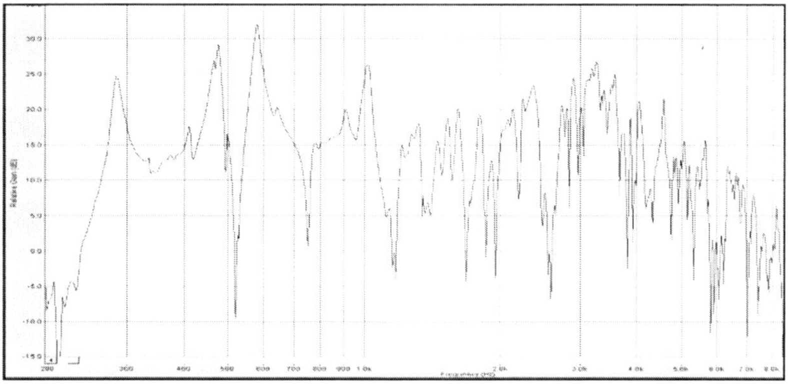

Fig. 4-14: Transfer function of a violin (Joseph Curtin, Luthier, 2009).

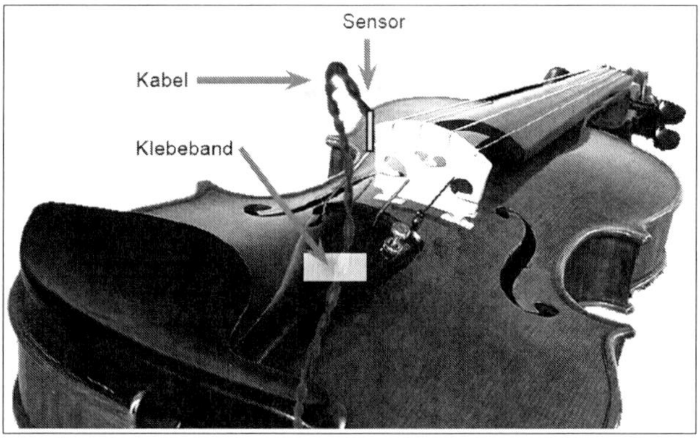

Fig. 4-15: Setup for an admittance measurement. The instrument gets excited at the right upper edge of the bridge by an impulse hammer. A sensor at the left side of the bridge records the reaction of the instrument.

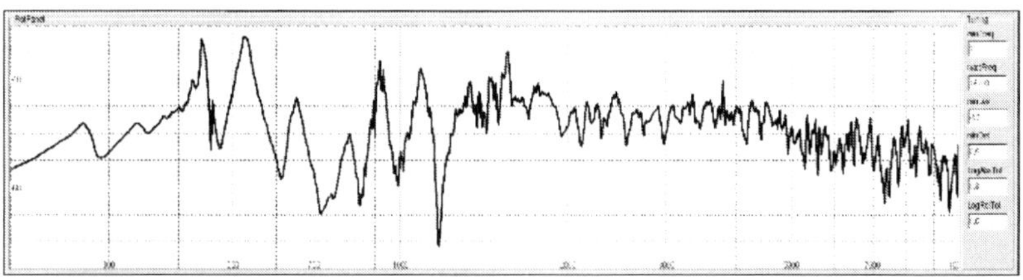

Fig. 4-16: Admittance curve of a violin.

Although a transfer function contains all information on the radiated sound of an instrument, it gives no information on the involved parts of the instrument. As string instruments (also pianos) consist of a multitude of parts which can influence the sound and response, a further method is required to clear up which part influences which of the radiated frequency. The solutions are measurements by Laser Hologram Interferometry or Electronic Speckle Pattern Interferometry. Both methods show which parts of the instrument are involved, and how much. In the early 70s, E. Jansson et al. were the first to carry out this work, and subsequently, Laser Holography, Interferometry or ESPI methods have commonly been used for all musical instruments, especially for pianos (see Figure 4-17).

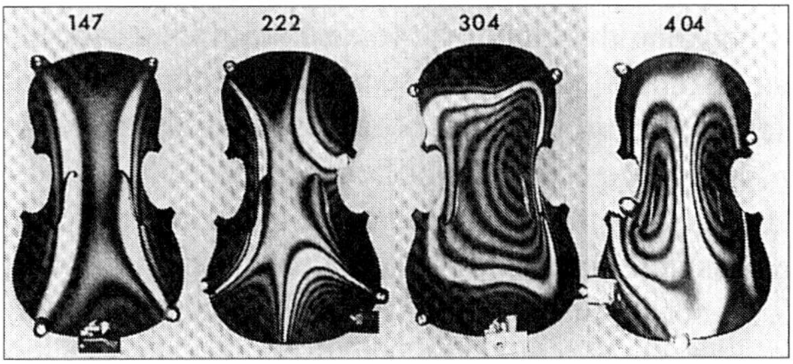

Fig. 4-17: Some vibration modes of a violin top plate by Erik Jansson et al. 1970.

Significantly greater computing power now enables us to use the Finite Element Method for investigating or improving stringed instruments. The figure below shows an early example by Antoine Chaigne (2003) for an acoustic guitar body (see Figure 4-18).

Fig. 4-18: Screenshots from the top plate movement of a guitar. Finite Element Simulation by Antoine Chaigne.

Today's state of knowledge enables any interested instrument maker to produce top class instruments, provided that he is willing to forget traditional myths and is open-minded enough to use the tools of our times and not those of the 19th century. Monitoring the international musical instrument maker scene shows that brass wind instrument makers and companies with mass production tend to accept and use new findings (about 100 BIAS systems are in use worldwide), whilst luthiers seem to be immune to new knowledge and modern tools. An explanation could be that in case of the violin, the number of parts with an influence on the timbre and response is much higher than in the case of brass instruments. Contrary to wind instruments, at least two different measurement methods are required.

Physiological Acoustics

The human ear, as the most important interface between the player and his instrument, can confidently be named as the world's most perfect microphone – but sometimes it has a will of its own and for musicians, the answer to the question: 'Can I trust my ears?' is: 'Yes and No'!

For example, in some cases we hear sounds which do not exist, and conversely, existing sounds are not perceived. Additionally, the perception of pitch is influenced by the loudness, and the impression of the loudness of a musical sound is not based (as one would think) on the sound level, but primary on the timbre!

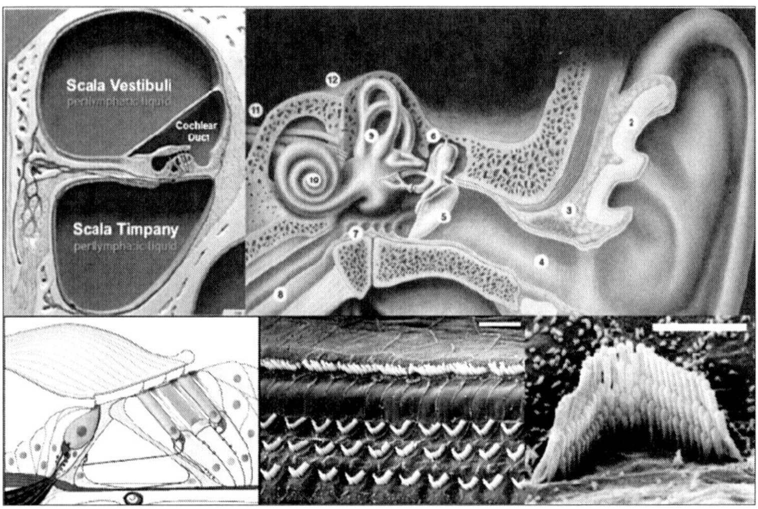

Fig. 4-19: From left to right: upper part: cross section of the cochlea, the whole ear. Lower part: Corti organ, outer and inner hair cells, hairs of an outer hair cell.

Our knowledge today about the function of the human ear is based on the investigations of the famed Georg von Békésy (1899-1972) and was significantly deepened in the last ten years by industrial cochlear implant research (see Figure 4-19). Basic information on the function of the human ear can be found here: http://www.neuroreille.com/promenade/english/ and http://www.cochlea.eu/en.

Psychoacoustics

Psychoacoustics is a sub-discipline of Psychophysics and investigates the relation between the perception of sounds and their acoustical properties. In other words: the relation between stimulus and sensation. As music exists only in our brain (before that, it is only patterns of various time-variant frequencies), psychoacoustics is an essential part of music acoustics and mainly deals with the data processing in our brains. On the journey from the cochlea to the brain, the digitally coded information passes various nodes consisting of a conglomeration of neurons (varying from ~30,000-500,000 neurons) where various aspects are 'preprocessed'; for example, the localization left-right-ahead at the Superior Olivary Complex. The first main stage in data processing is done by the Primary Auditory Cortex (~100 million neurons).

Although new discoveries are published nearly every month, more questions are still open than answered. Aside from some well-known hearing phenomena like 'template matching' which results from efficiency reasons – the incoming neuronal patterns are not always analyzed but only compared to the stored templates in the cortex – we know that making music can cause significant changes in the brain.

Neuroplasticity

This phenomenon, well understood for ten years, occurs if one uses specific synapses many thousands of times, leading to the growth of new synapses and finally new neurons. For example, the brain region responsible for the movement of the fingers of the left hand of violin players is 1.5-3.0 cms larger than that of normal people. Additionally, all professional musicians have a significantly larger and better working Corpus Callosum (connects the left and right hemisphere). This is because playing music in a professional manner also involves the left (analytical) hemisphere, in contrast to laypersons where mainly the holistic right hemisphere is involved.

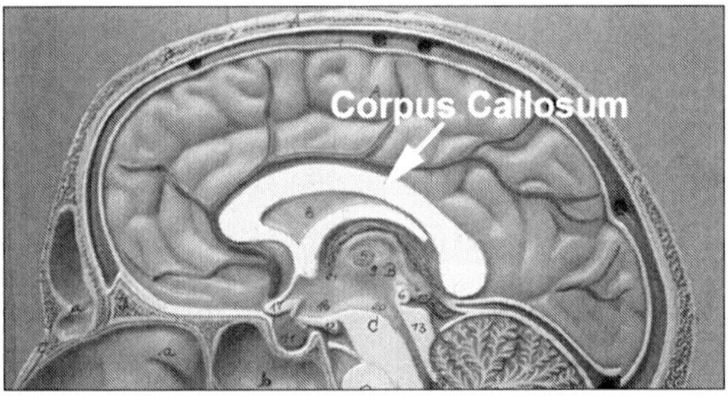

Fig. 4-20: An increased Corpus Callosum in the brain of professional musicians provides a significantly better crosslinking.

An interesting phenomenon where no satisfactory explanation has existed until now is the relationship between a low laterality and an increased 'left handedness' (see Table 1).

Table 1. Percentage of left handed persons.

	Musician	**Non-Musician**
Male	**12.2%**	**8.5%**
Female	**11.8%**	**7.2%**

Performance Science

Performance science is the latest discipline and started officially in 2007 with its first international congress in Porto (Portugal). As well as acoustical aspects it also covered medical topics like musicians' health and typical musicians' diseases (all sorts of focal dystonia, stage fright, and problems with the musculoskeletal system) as well as applied performance psychology and physiology.

It should be mentioned that research projects in Performance Science mostly require an increased expenditure for measurement equipment, because measured data using many diverse sensors have to be set into relationship and synchronized. In my presentation, I will discuss research results which predominantly outline acoustical aspects.

The following movie screenshots (see Figure 4-21 and Figure 4-22) are an example of realtime capturing of all of the parameters of violin playing as they are: involved string(s), bow position, bow angle, bow velocity and bow pressure as well as the movement of the shoulders, head, upper arm and forearm, wrist and position of the fingers. Such investigations require specific sensors and the application of a motion capture system. Besides the gain of new scientific insights, the application of such methods can be very useful in cases where a teacher can hardly explicitly identify the technical problems of students. Such a research project with violin players was done for the first time at McGill University (Canada) and at the KTH (Schoonderwaldt 2010).

Similar investigations concerning the piano playing took place in Montreal and Vienna (Goebl et al. 2009 and 2010), between 2006 and 2012. The main questions were: How do movement patterns change with performance rate? What are the consequences of different types of touch e.g. 'struck' (from above) or 'pressed' (finger resting at the surface)?

Another focus can be the analysis of individual stylistic aspects of famous pianists and the comparison with other top international players (Goebl et al. 2009, Grachten et al. 2009) (see Figure 4-23 and Figure 4-24).

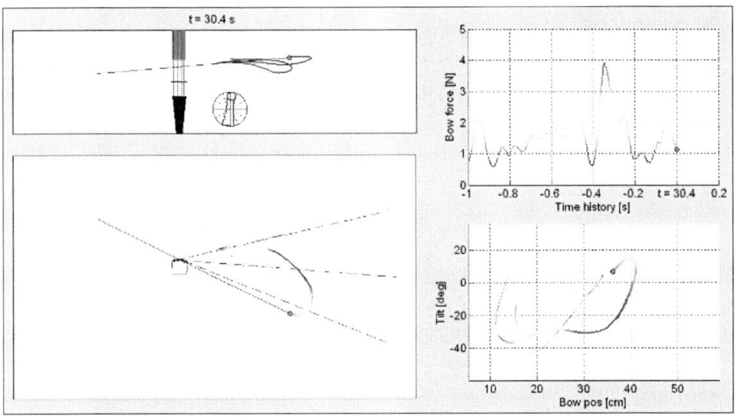

Fig. 4-21: Violin playing parameter (screenshot). Upper left: used string, bow angle at string contact point, bow position and angle in the horizontal plain; lower left: bow angle in the vertical plain; upper right: bow force versus time; lower right: bow position versus tilt.

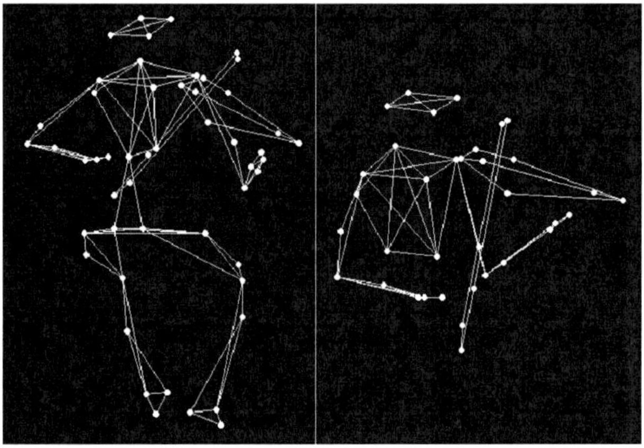

Fig. 4-22: Sensor arrangement of the motion capture system.

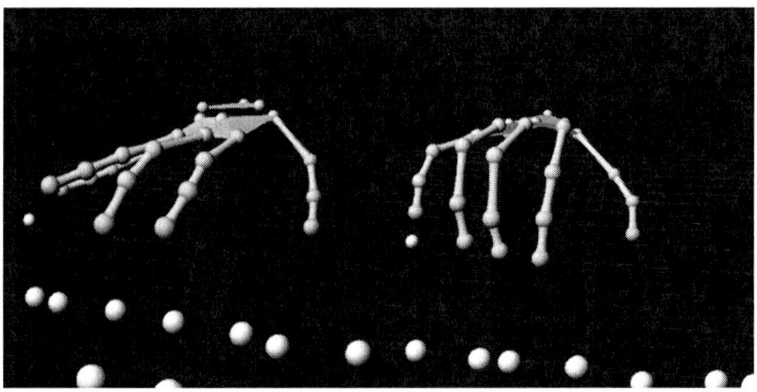

Fig. 4-23: Different types of touch. Left: pressed; right: struck.

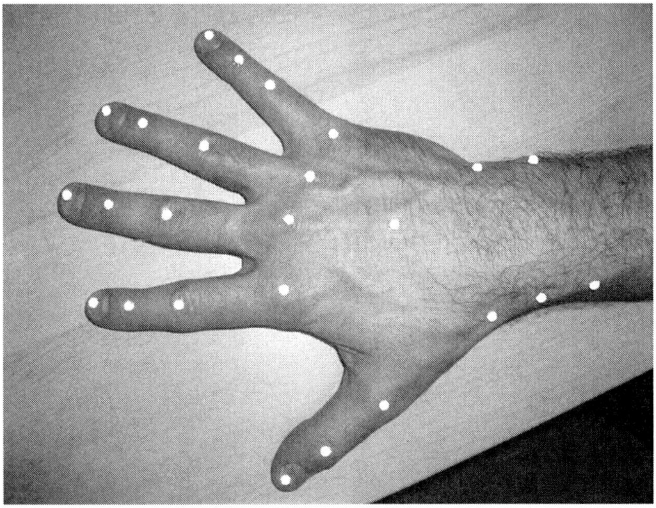

Fig. 4-24: Arrangement of the sensors for piano playing measurements.

Conclusion

Music Acoustics is a highly inter-disciplinary science. Depending on the object of research, its main focus can be physics, mathematics, physiology, psychology, neuroscience, brain research or even medical sciences.

Its target audience is accordingly diverse: it varies from scientists, musicians and teachers to health professionals.

The reasons for its relatively late establishment as an independent field of science were:

- the lack of adequate technical equipment
- insufficient computing power and
- too few people who understand both the language of scientists and artists

To achieve practice-oriented results, Music Acoustics often uses methods from other sciences and/or even depends on these results. Due to the fact that the objects under investigation are mostly new and unusual, it requires in the majority of cases new, unorthodox and often transdisciplinary methods. Working in the field of Music Acoustics means to be highly communicative by nature. A side effect of that is the creation of many newly developed, particular and sophisticated software tools free for researchers of other sciences via open source libraries. The growing interest in cooperation on the part of musicians is evident, whilst the behaviour of instrument makers is ambivalent: the majority of wind instrument makers are interested in new knowledge and the use of modern tools, whilst luthiers react to the offer of music acousticians in general with anxiety and deprecation. There are two exceptions worldwide: the luthiers Martin Schleske (Germany) who studied physics, and Joseph Curtin (USA). They have done a lot of research themselves and use the methods described in this paper for their work with great worldwide success.

A survey of the entire area of research shows that Musical Instrument Research is the most advanced sub-discipline already producing commercial tools, as far as instrument customizing and cloning tools is concerned. Physiological Acoustics has been advanced by cochlear implant and hearing aid research while Psychoacoustics, depending on the success of brain research and caused by an extremely high level of complexity, has the greatest number of open questions. Performance Science is the 'baby' of the sub-disciplines and is characterized by rapid progress.

References

Benade, A. (1969). *Fundamentals of Musical Acoustics, New York.*

—. (1977). *The Physics of Wood Winds* (KENT, Earle L., Stroudsburg/PA). 265-273.

—. (1983). *Air column, reed, and player's windway interaction in musical instruments*. Czechosl. Scient. & Techn. Society, Hradec Králové. 113-168.

Chaine A., et al. (2003*). Numerical Simulation of the Acoustic Guitar.* DVD by INRA, France.

Chatziioannou, V., Kausel, W., Moore, T. (2012). *The effect of wall vibrations on the air column inside trumpet bells*. Proceedings of the Acoustics 2012 Nantes Conference (Nantes, France). 2243-2248.

Chatziioannou, V., van Walstijn M. (2012) *Estimation of Clarinet Reed Parameters by Inverse Modelling*. Acta Acustica, Vol. 98 No. 4629-639(11).

Dalmont, J., Gilbert, and S. Oliver. (2003). *Nonlinear characteristics of single-reed instruments: Quasi-static volume flow and reed opening measurements.* J. Acoust. Soc. Am. 114, 2253-2262.

Goebl, W.; Palmer, C. (2010) *Analyzing finger motion in piano performance: Touch and tempo effects.* Proceedings of the Second Vienna Talk on Music Acoustics.

—. (2009) *Finger motion in piano performance: Touch and tempo.* International Symposium on Performance Science (ISPS), Auckland, New Zealand, edited by Williamon, (AEC), Utrecht, The Netherlands, 65-70.

Goebl, W.; Widmer, G. (2009) *On the use of computational methods for expressive music performance, in Modern Methods for Musicology: Prospects, Proposals, and Realities.* Ashgate Publishing, London, 93-113.

Goebl, W.; Palmer, C. (2009) *Synchronization of timing and motion among performing musicians.* Music Perception 26, 427-438.

Goebl, W.; Pampalk, E.; Widmer, G. (2004) *Exploring expressive performance trajectories: Six famous pianists play six Chopin piece.* Proceedings of the 8th International Conference on Music Perception and Cognition, 505-509.

Guillemain Ph. (2004). *A Digital Synthesis Model of Double-Reed Wind Instruments.* EURASIP Journal on Advances in Signal Processing, 990-1000.

Grachten, M.; Goebl, W.; Flossmann, S.; Widmer, G. (2009) *Phase-plane representation and visualization of gestural structure in expressive timing.* Journal of New Music Research 38, 183-195.

Hofmann, A., Chatziioannou, V., Kausel, W., Goebl, W., Weilguni, M., Smetana, W. (2012). *The influence of tonguing on tone production with single-reed instruments.* 5th Congress of the Alps Adria Acoustics Association (Petrcane (Zadar), Croatia), to appear.

Jansson, E.; Molin, N.- E.; Sundin, H. (1970 / 1976) *Resonances of a Violin Body Studied by Hologram Interferometry and Acoustical Methods.* Phys. Scr. 2, 1970, p. 243, and Stroudsburg/PA, 1976, 131-144.

Kausel, W., Anglmayer, P. (1999) *A Computer Program for Brass Instrument Optimization – Part I. Concept and Implementation.* In Proceedings of the 137th Meeting of the ASA and 2nd Convention of the EAA Forum Acusticum (Berlin).

Kausel, W. (2001) *Bore reconstruction from measured acoustical input impedance: equipment, signal processing, algorithms and prerequisites.* In Proceedings of ISMA 2, 373-378.

—. (2001). *Optimization of Brasswind Instruments and its Application in Bore Reconstruction.* Journal of New Music Research. 69-82.

Kausel, W., Moore, T. (2010) *Coupling between air column and structural vibrations in the flaring bell of brass wind instruments*. Journal of the Acoustical Society of America (JASA) 128, 2419.

Kausel, W., Zietlow, D., Moore, T. (2010). *Influence of wall vibrations on the sound of brass wind instruments*. Journal of the Acoustical Society of America 128, 3161-3174.

Kühnelt, H. (2003). *Simulating the mechanism of sound generation in flutes using the lattice Boltzmann method.* Proceedings of the SMAC03 (Stockholm Music Acoustics Conference), Royal Swedish Academy of Music, Stockholm, 401-404.

Mapes-Riordan, D. (1993). *Horn Modeling with Conical and Cylindrical Transmission-Line Elements*. In Journal of the Audio Engineering Society 41, 471-483.

Schoonderwaldt E. (2010) *Control and Coordination of Complex Bowing Patterns.* Proceedings of the Second Vienna Talk on Music Acoustics, 133-136.

Widholm, G. (1995). *Brass wind instrument quality measured and evaluated by a new computer system*. Proceedings of the 15th International Congress on Acoustics, Trondheim (N), 517-520.
http://artim.at/?page_id=5&sprache=2

European Acoustics Association, TC Musical Acoustics, Workgroup 2.
https://www.euracoustics.org/technical-committees/tc-on-musical-acoustics

http://www.schleske.de/en/our-research.html. This website offers a complete bundle of lectures on all aspects of violin acoustics and instrument making.

CHAPTER FIVE

MUSIC PERFORMANCE AND INTERACTIONS: *A CHANGING LANDSCAPE*. AN EXPERIENCE OF AUDIOVISUAL INSTALLATION

SIMONETTA SARGENTI
CONSERVATORIO DI MUSICA "G. ROSSINI", PESARO

Introduction

This paper, and the considerations contained with it, originate from an experience of the composition of background music for a project of architectural regeneration that later became, in different performances, an audio-visual installation with its own independent character. So it is therefore an interdisciplinary project in which the musical idea was born out of the established belief that the perception of a landscape doesn't involve only the elements of visual and spatial character, but also the sound elements that compose the landscape. The soundscape is an integral part of our perception of the landscape in general.

In the composition described in the present paper, the sounds accompanying the viewing were, in part, sounds from the landscape itself and, in part, realized through synthetic instruments and techniques. The perception of the whole depends on the interaction with the movements of those who observe and listen. This way, the concepts of relationship between sound and image and between sound and listening space also come into play. By now, technologies have for a long time been contributing to the rethinking of these relationships as well as to their use in both musical and multimedia compositions.

Aims of the project

Starting from reflections about the meaning of gestural expressiveness in sound production and the relationship of the latter with the sound result, I created and carried out some experiences of interactive composition and improvisation in which the role of the interpreter could have an influence in various ways on the outcome of the composition.

In this specific context, through this project, I would like to deepen my reflection on how interactive technologies keep facilitating the spread of the use of certain aspects of artistic and musical composition such as, in the first place, a) sound-space interaction, and b) the interpreter-listener/observer relationship.

The audio-visual installation *A changing landscape* was quite a simple experiment with interaction. However, it enabled me to create a relationship between different ambits, starting from the coupling of music with an architectural project of landscape regeneration. The initial proposal consisted in creating background music for a project involving the regeneration of a landscape. Therefore, it was a musical work born in the context of the redesigning of a space that supplied the starting point for the in depth study of the interaction between sound and environment. The idea of proposing the form of the audio-visual installation derived exactly from the fact that the project was going to be enjoyed through the listener-spectator's experience of the space. The interactive technologies, in this case of the relationship between presence-movement and the sound-visual outcome, highlight the importance of the interpreter-spectator-observer relationship.

The audio-visual installation, although it started from the original idea of the landscape's regeneration, would later also be realized separately from it and performed in other contexts as a stand-alone musical and visual installation. In this form, it was performed on June 23, 2009 in Milano, at the Villa Simonetta.

Project references

Architectural references. The idea of *A changing landscape* was, from its inception, linked to an architectural project of the regeneration of some mines that had been worked on in South-Western Sardinia. Some images of the landscape are shown in Figure 5-1, Figure 5-2 and Figure 5-

3. The first picture shows an image of one of these ancient mines; the second picture shows the village of Porto Flavia, one location of the mines; and third picture shows a natural landscape surrounding the village.

A first reference for this idea of background music was the project by the Centro de Investigacion Sonora of the Jardin de San Francisco in Madrid, realised by the Spanish architect Pablo A. Padilla Jargstorf in 2005. In it, some thin vegetable sheets with different bends produce different acoustic responses depending on the visitors' placement within the space. Here the concept of soundscape is conceived as the 'primordial element of the comprehension of our surroundings, always implied in our visual experience, that plays a fundamental role in our spatial perception' (Padilla Jargstorf, 2005).

Fig. 5-1: Image of the ancient mine.

Fig. 5-2: The ancient mining village of Porto Flavia.

Fig. 5-3: The natural landscape of Porto Flavia.

A second reference for the interactive composition of the music for *A changing landscape* were the theories by French architect Gilles Clément, expounded in his main works and, in particular, in his *Manifesto of the third landscape.* To build a garden we need to observe that, 'The space-garden should be lived and observed as the place of the change where "some biological energy unfolds naturally"' and 'experimentation in the garden is to leave all things as they are' (Clément, 2004).

Musical references. The main musical reference for the composition of *A changing landscape* was the conception of the sound expressed by Luigi Nono in his late works composed with live electronic techniques; for example, *Prometeo* a work for solo voices, chorus and orchestra or *A Pierre dell'azzurro silenzio inquietum* for flute and live electronics, and *La lontananza nostalgica utopica futura* for violin and tape. In all his works from the 80s, the compositions are the result of the research of the sound composer and performer who have a continuous interaction; they are "caminantes without caminos" as the composer himself described in the foreword of the score, *La lontananza* (Nono, 1989):

> In the performing space, the sounds change according to the points of listening and the performer's ideas. We never have equal performances.

Elements of the composition

Visual elements. The visual part of *A changing landscape* is composed of a series of images chosen from a group of photos of seascapes, arid lands, and wooded areas from the original architectural landscape regeneration project. You can see some examples in the following pictures:

Fig. 5-4: Image of wooded areas.

Fig. 5-5: Image of arid land.

Fig. 5-6: Image of seascape.

Sound elements. Each type of image is combined with different audio files composed with the sounds of acoustic instruments, with synthetic sounds, and with sounds from the landscape itself. You can hear them in the following audio examples (listen CD-ROM sound files 05, 06 and 07): a) instrumental sound; b) synthetic sound; c) sound of landscape (sea sound).

Spatial elements. The installation is arranged in such a way as to be performed along a spatial route of a size between 5 and 8 metres in length, like a corridor, a room or a courtyard, outdoor or indoor. Within this space, the images are projected and at the same time the audio files are played. By walking through the installation area, each visitor-listener will be presented with different perspectives of the images and of the accompanying sounds. Figure 5-7 shows the space where the installation was performed in concert on June 23, 2009 at the Villa Simonetta in Milano.

Element of interaction and technical realisation

The changes during the running of the installation depend on two types of events: a) number of spectators present, and b) type of movements of the spectators.

The presence of the public and their movements are detected by a video camera and affect the transformation of the sounds and images, which are processed by an algorithm realized through the program max/msp.

In Figure 5-8, you can see the algorithm of the installation: a video camera captures the images of people; the algorithm calculates the values of brightness, contrast and saturation and sends them to control the audio and video. In this way audio files and the landscape's images are modified during the performance.

A relationship between the different elements of the installation is the main idea of the composition. At the starting point of the whole composition, there are the following connections:

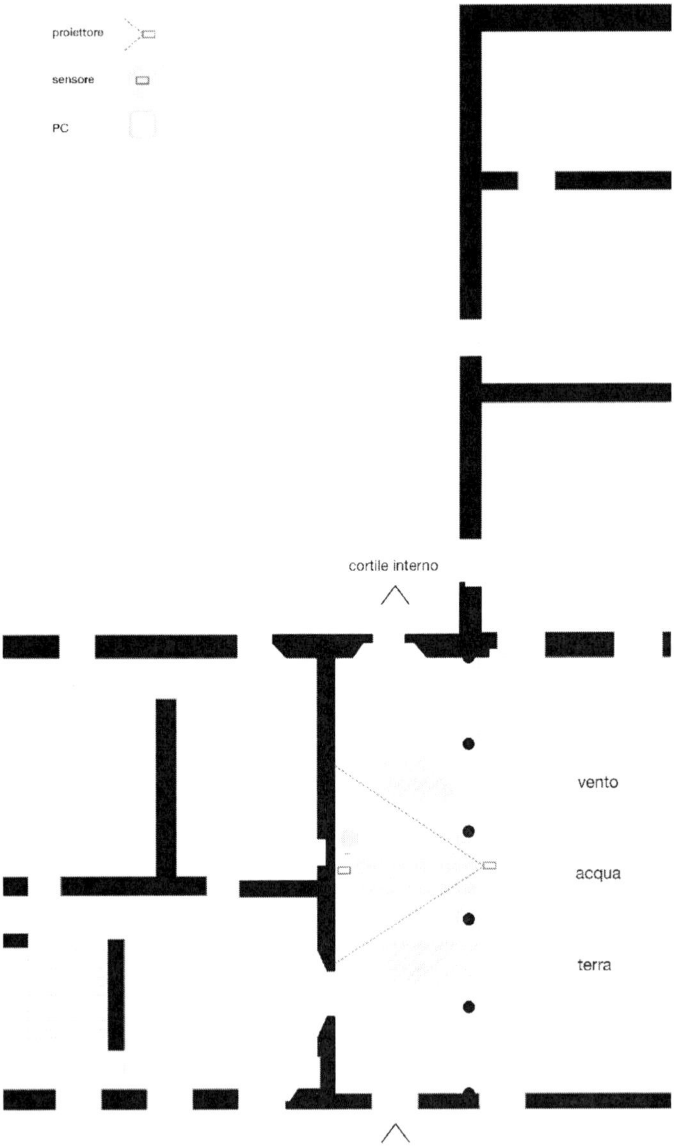

Fig. 5-7: Example of a performing space.

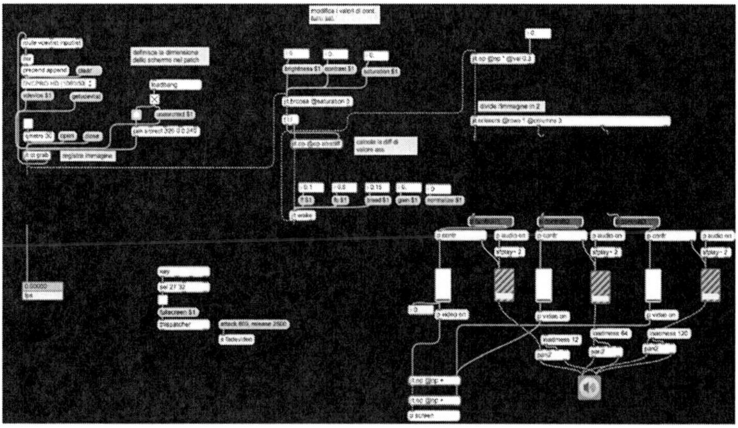

Fig. 5-8: The algorithm of *A changing landscape.*

A time connection in which the past is associated with the ruins of the ancient mines, the present with the natural seascape and the future with a regenerated landscape (the landscape of the architectural project). In the installation, the future can be also associated with the image of the wooded area. The images are then related with the different kinds of sounds: metallic sounds produced with synthesis, natural sounds produced from the seascape, and instrumental sounds (see Table 5-1).

The installation is running when the people come in. If it is on, but no-one comes inside the performance space, then we have a total absence of sound and vision. When spectators enter, the audio and video start to run. At the beginning of the performance, we can see images and hear sounds with the initial relation as shown in Table 5-1.

As summarised in Table 5-2, if we don't have people in the area of the projection of music and video, we have darkness and silence and nothing happens. With a minimal presence of spectators, we start to hear audio and to see images. The sequence of images and the combination of sounds depends on the presence of viewers and listeners in the area.

Table 5-1. Sound-image associations at the beginning of the composition.

TIME	Past	Present	Future
IMAGE	Landscape with ruins	Natural seascape	Regenerated landscape
	Rocks, arid land	Sea, beach	Wood, wind
MUSIC	Metallic sounds	Water sounds	Acoustic instruments
	Sounds of recorded instruments	Water sounds from the seascape	Synthetic sounds

Table 5-2. Changes produced on images and sounds from the presence of people in the performance space.

Total absence of spectators and therefore of movement	Darkness and silence
Minimal presence of spectators	Start of sounds and images
Increase in presence of spectators	More changes in sounds and images
Maximum presence of spectators	Maximum changes in sounds and images

Conclusions

The project offered here is an opportunity to deepen our reflection on various topical themes:

1. Interaction as an emerging element of many current artistic activities that are being made available as a result of increasingly improving technologies.

2. The function of the interpreter who, in the final analysis, can even be the spectators themselves or a person acting from a distance. Also on this point, if at the dawn of the use of live electronics there was an interaction, for example, between the performers on their

instruments and the composer's about through the way the sound was produced by the performer and processed by the sound engineer, with interaction, this process now also extends to the spectator-listener.

3. Furthermore, still through interaction techniques, it is possible to deepen the interrelation existing in this type of work between sound and visual event, as well as between space and movement, putting into practice an interdisciplinary principle.

4. *A changing landscape* is therefore not particularly innovative from a technical point of view, but it enabled me to deepen different ambits of disciplines: music and architecture, video and audio composition, sound and space relations. Therefore it is a music composition born out of a context in which the idea of an audiovisual installation becomes a composition independent even from the original context. Finally, in it, interaction is a medium of interrelation between different subjects in the artistic expression, where technology allows one to obtain interesting results.

References

Murray Schaefer R. 1985. *The tuning of the world*, Italian edition: *Il paesaggio sonoro*. Milano: Ricordi unicopli.

Sargenti S. 2012. Gesture and sound analysis: virtual instruments for an interactive composition. *Proceedings of EMS12*, Stockholm. Online publication: www.ems-network.org/ems12

Padilla Jargstorf P. A. 2009. *Proyecto por la realization sonora del jardin de S. Francisco en Madrid.* Madrid: ESAYA (Escuela Superior de Arte y Architectura).

Clément G. 2005. *Manifeste du tierce paysage*, Italian edition: Il manifesto del terzo paesaggio. Macerata: Quodlibet.

Nono L. 2001. *Scritti e colloqui,* a cura di A. I. De Benedictis e V. Rizzardi. Milano: Lucca.

CHAPTER SIX

COMPOSITIONAL PROCESS ANALYSIS OF THE ORIGINAL ALBUM *SCOPES AND PLATFORMS*

NERINGA ŽALTAUSKAITĖ
KAUNAS UNIVERSITY OF TECHNOLOGY

Introduction

The category of 'experimental' refers to the great discoveries of the pioneers in electronic music genres. Where composition incorporates both directing and producing with the technologies and exploration, the musical work has so many stages that it becomes vital to separate the different elements of composition, while maintaining the solid interrelations.

Since the project scheduling and planning resulted in advanced and challenging design, projection and preparation, the questioning of aesthetics was explored while the project was in process. Hence, the discourse of the connections between all the influences and their results, while taking the tendencies and techniques into consideration, will be presented in the sections designated for the research and project implementation description.

Experiments with electronic music in general began with the electronic inventions and technological progress in the 19th century, which proves the significance of the link between music and history. As the constantly growing research in music composition looks back to the needs of live music performances in the classical music scene, while composers were trying to stand out with their artistic touch and convey social messages, modern composers still adapt and improve the traditional methods and are still looking for new collaborations with other artistic forms. During the years of constant change and encounters with various social and political circumstances, compositional tendencies have been adapted to specific conditions and social settings, and modified due to various musical applications. Furthermore, music composition has been explored by sound engineers who base their work on listening skills. This gave an entirely new direction for sound art and has resulted in innovative scientific fields and research purposes that have brought sound art to the state of sound composition as an art form perceived from the five viewpoints of sound quality, characteristics, potential, applications, musical implications and more. This instantly suggests constant improvements of musical techniques. In this report, the most common composition techniques and jazz style features that were applied to the process of making *Scopes and Platforms* will be described.

The research subject

At the very first stage of this solo project, the main object of research was meant to be the album itself and an explanation of its compositional process. However, due to the many aspects of creativity, the research subject was changed from the album itself to the composition of the album.

The research area

The research had seven main areas of focus: the fields of composition, contemporary jazz, electronic music, music psychology, performance practice, improvisation and granular synthesis. The research done in these areas and its related aspects provided additional directions for the music aesthetics discussion, which also relates to research in sound and music aesthetics. Thus, due to the interaction of composition methods and sound production techniques, the research was expanded to consider the connection between sound and music.

Literature review

To date, no research in contemporary electronic experimental composition has integrated microsound and mainstream western musical styles, such as jazz, despite microsound having become a staple approach in the contemporary electronic music scene. This study aims to pursue the connection of the most unique sound features of the genres and to investigate the nature of the composition process in a folio of compositions called *Scopes and Platforms.* So while writing the master thesis, the research was done with regard to the related topics and musical works, based on the existing literature on postmodern and modern music, its techniques and aesthetics.

Both electronic music and jazz composition techniques are united and employed by working with performing musicians. This allows the project to also consider collaboration with people from different musical backgrounds, to incorporate their experience of listening and performing practice. It also encourages the exploration of sonic features in specific instrumental playing, such as the relation to a particular playing style and rules, or neglecting both. As any criterion of subjective judgment has been eliminated during the implementation of this project, the decisions have only been based upon aesthetic ideas defined by respected composers, musicologists and other researchers. These aesthetic ideas have enabled the links between the sound materials and the final album sound nature. The music was not composed merely by using the ideas learned from other researchers, but it was developed as a response to the combination of human psychology, aesthetic notions, contemporary and modern techniques, and improvisation practice. Moreover, some additional elements were used as inspirational sources to ignite the creative process.

The methods of research

The main research method in the experimental electronic music field was chosen to be the compositional process. While analysing its documentation, this kind of research also provides some information on the practical aspects of the matter, which, when combined with aesthetic considerations, enables a more powerful demonstration of the nature of sound, the importance of performance skills, technological influences, and how all these means could be innovatively combined.

Compositional development

During the composition of the pieces, some observations about the sound and music composition were made. The work and feedback showed that making a plan of a piece is crucial. Letting a plan change and involving spontaneity makes it challenging after the initial planning is done. However, composing music and composing sound are two very different notions that sometimes might assimilate into one, while music composition and sound composition are both used in the production of a piece. Moreover, let me underline the difference in the case of this album.

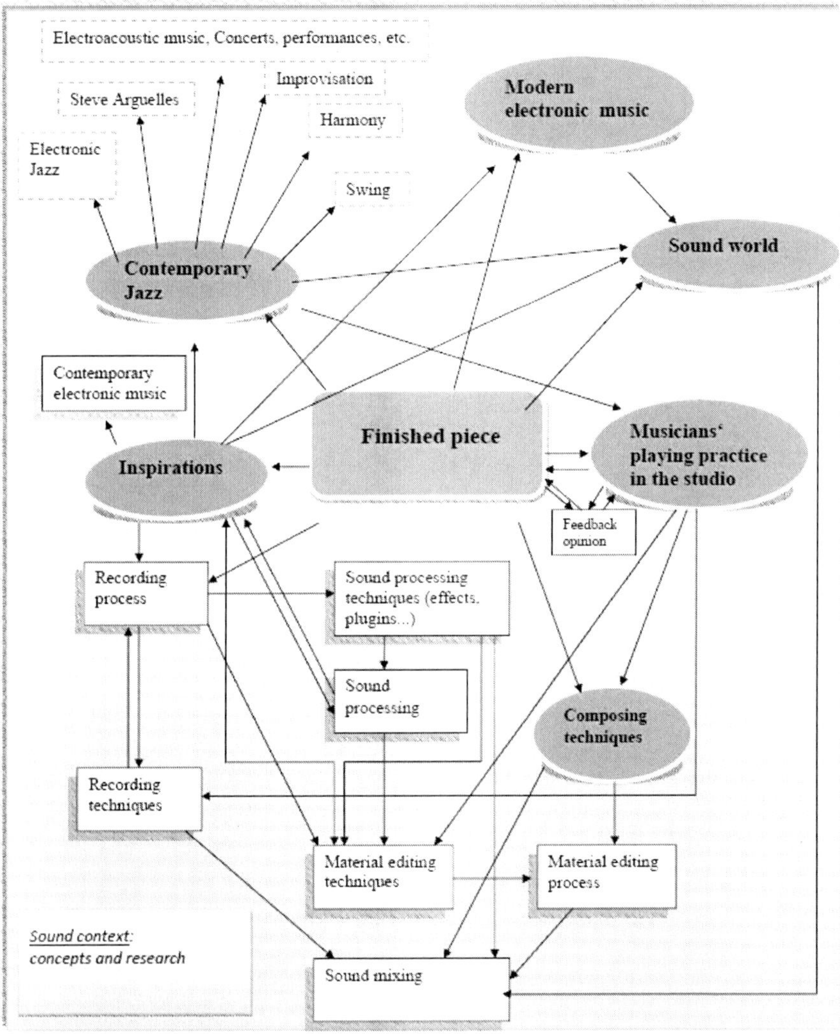

Fig. 6-1: Compositional Process Relationships.

By sound composition, I mean the compositional process of the sonic piece, which includes making sound quality decisions, aligning or distributing sounds and any further modifications performed, layering consequences and their result in the form of an experimentation, sound mixing and other related artistic sonic actions that refer to the sound quality and characteristics more than to the arrangement. By music composition, I mean the composing of the arrangement and instrumentation for the sound materials made beforehand. In order to describe the whole process successfully, it was important to research the stages and influences of the work separately. This is why the relationships between many influential aspects were described (see Figure 6-1).

While the compositional process was evolving, the organisation and the roles of sound elements were defined as well as the ways of creative thinking related to listening experiences. It was also very important to analyse the music relations to the sound world and sound context that also included the use of jazz notions, experimentations and improvisations. Most of the experiments took place in the music studio environment, where improvisation was applied together with electronic sound effects. As the sound of the album was crafted in the studio, a separate stage of work was devoted to the studio techniques that included granular synthesis applied to the acoustic jazz recordings and shaped into layers and textures afterwards. With relation to the music recordings, the performance practice in the studio environment proved the need for and benefits of feedback and the importance of the listening experience.

Aesthetic significance

The significance of music and sound aesthetics is such a large concept that it forces one to concentrate on specific examples of movements, traditions and conventions rather than on one specific type of sound of music. In relation to social changes and political reasons, aesthetics gain power that cannot be neglected. However, many aesthetic directions are often incorrectly understood and their terms are used for discussions of contemporary issues. Despite the evolving nature of electronic music concepts, the historical origins of aesthetic notions are yet still the most reliable. Suppose that aesthetic ideas come from three basic categories: cultural movements, compositional traditions and compositional conventions. Taking this further, the cultural movements involve the main origins of minimalism and surrealism that are closely related to this solo project's implementation, because of granular synthesis, musical influences and inspirations used. The compositional traditions and conventions could be mainly used as a niche for electronic music and experimental music concepts. While they create experimental prospects, the depiction of the notion of experimental music from the composer's viewpoint plays an important part in the realisation of this project in combination with scientific and technological inspiration. The project's commitments to surrealism, minimalism, microsound with sound morphology, the concept of electronic music, and experimental music aesthetics will be described in this chapter. Whether or not these concepts have much influence on the music composed is a subject for critical consideration, due to the possible delusions in creativity.

These are the reasons why the lines between the experimental music aesthetics and human sound perception become blurred and the concepts intertwine. However, analysing the sound morphology, and investigating the contemporary jazz and microsound aesthetics relationships could give some relevant background to the research of the compositional process as it outlined the limits of the created sound. Here the scientific works that have researched noise and failure come into consideration. As every sound aspect might have had some aesthetic influence, the project was considerably shaped according to aspects of the research area.

Design and methodology of the research

The form of a sonic album was chosen as a design of research for several reasons. Firstly, it demands consistency and requires novelty. Secondly, it sets some boundaries as the experimentation should find its logical place among other recognised musical works. And thirdly, such a model gives many directions for research, starting from musicology and going towards psychoacoustics.

The methodology of the research was not chosen to be as varied as it appeared to be. Starting with the methods of collecting the data that was analysed later, the impact on different aspects was lessened as it was working both ways (see Figure 6-2). At first, some electronic music spectral data was intended to be produced. But during the composing process, such a method of analysis appeared to be too narrow and too rigorous. It also would have made the analysis pointless, because the sound materials involved so many different aesthetic meanings that incorporated ideas rather than technology itself. So, the methods of analysis depended more on the nature of the data. Therefore, data was collected in the form of a composition diary, score writing, and recordings of music (see Figure 6-2), which helped to realise each benefit for each stage of work. Then the aesthetic analysis was applied, regarding the recognised sources. Such a method of analysis corresponds with the idea of a free improvised experiment very well.

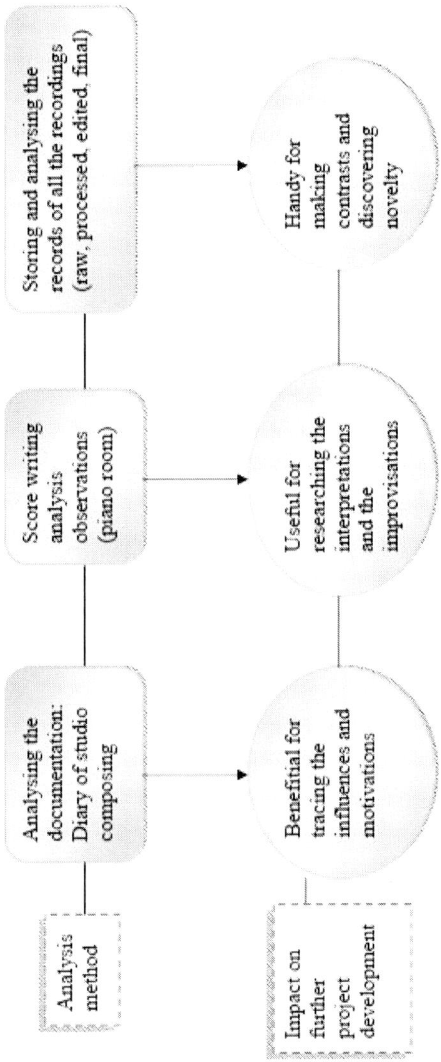

Fig. 6-2: Methods of collecting data.

The presentation of analysis and data is verbal and refers to primary sources as the compositions were described by the composer and the documentation was made during the creative process. The outcomes of the analysis had some impact on the development of the project, because it was carried out while the project was in progress. Thus, this analysis can be considered to be more of an observation than an objective investigation.

Outcomes and findings

During the implementation of the project, three original experimental pieces were composed, compared and analysed. The first piece was called 'Watermarking' and demonstrated the sonic possibilities of a combination of jazzy guitar and piano parts that were granularized, processed, and mixed using a Microsound aesthetic reference. The second, 'Under', exposed flute and double bass tracks that were composed as a jazzy duet, where the interaction between the instruments was shaped into an orchestral sound space. The third piece, 'Stuffed animals', demonstrated the use of improvisation influences on the initial written scores while recording the tracks, while the sound reference made the resulting sound very focused.

The project has proved the importance of feedback to the listening experience as well as the importance of listening while composing. Furthermore, the innovative relationship between the prospects of the sound materials and the aesthetic possibilities implied by many related influences was discovered due to the many relationships between the sound components. This has led to a great distinction between the sound of the album and the sound contexts of the pieces, which can be described as making a niche in the innovative experimental music context, because of the unique combination of sound elements and the musical concepts employed (listen to the CD-ROM sound files 08, 09 and 10).

References

Anon. 'Steve Arguelles'. URL: <http://www.jazzcds.co.uk/artist_id_12/biography_id_12> [last accessed 28 August 2012].

Bailey, D. 1992. *Improvisation.* London, The British National Sound Archive.

Cascone, Kim. 2012. 'The aesthetics of failure: "Post-digital" tendencies in contemporary computer music'. URL: <http://mitpress.mit.edu/journals/comj/cmj24_4cascone.pdf>

In *Computer Music Journal* [last accessed 29 August 2012].
Cole, B. 1996. *The composer's handbook.* London, Schott Educational.
Cox, C. & Warner, D. 2004. *Audio culture: readings in modern music.* New York, London, Continuum.
Dankworth, A. 1968. *Jazz. An introduction to its musical basic*s. London, Oxford University Press.
Demers, J. 2012. *Listening through noise: the aesthetics of experimental electronic music.* Oxford, Oxford University Press.
Dodge, C. & Jerse, T. A. 1985. *Computer music.* New York, Schirmer Books.
Emerson, S. 1986. *The language of electroacoustic music.* New York, Harwood Academic Publishers.
Goldstein, G. 1993. *Jazz composers' companion.* Rottenburg, Advance Music.
Holmes, T. 2002. *Electronic and experimental music.* New York and London, Routledge.
Huron, D. 2006. *Sweet anticipation.* London, MIT Press.
LeBaron, A. 2001. *Reflections of surrealism in postmodern music.* New York, Garland Press.
Lippe, C. 1994. 'Real-time Granular Sampling Using the IRCAM Signal Processing Workstation'. *Contemporary Music Review.* Paris, Harwood Academic Publishers.
Lockhead, J. & Auner, J. 2002. *Postmodern music/Postmodern thought.* New York and London, Routledge.
Lyon, J. 'The contemporary jazz sound'. URL: <http://www.opus28.co.uk/jazzarticles.html> [last accessed 29 August 2012].
Nyman, M. 1999. *Experimental Music*. Cambridge, Cambridge University Press.
Porto, E. 2002. *What is this thing called jazz?* Berkeley, Los Angeles, London, University of California Press.
Roads, C. 2004. *Microsound*. London, MIT Press.
—. 1997. *Musical signal processing*. Exton, PA, Swets & Zeitlinger.
Ross, A. 1968. *The rest is noise.* London, Harper Perennial.
Sloboda, J.A. 2000. *Generative processes in music.* New York, Oxford University Press.
Smalley, D. 1978. *Electroacoustic composition.* Unpubl. DPhil thesis, University of York.
—. 'Spectromorphology: Explaining Sound-Shapes'. URL: <https://www.city.ac.uk/arts/academic-staff-profiles/professor-denis-smalley> in *Organised Sound* [last accessed 29 August 2012].

Wilson, S. 2006. *In defense of contemporary electronic music*. Master's thesis, Wichita State University.

Musical Sources

Air. 'Alone in Kyoto'. URL: <http://www.youtube.com/watch?v=jC1tIfoYjwo> (version current at 26 August 2012).

Bjork. 'Oceania'. URL: <http://www.youtube.com/watch?v=cGCKPt1SlF0> [last accessed 28 August 2012].

Boards of Canada. 'Left side drive'. URL: <http://www.youtube.com/watch?v=f0tbuZgjqJc> [last accessed 28 August 2012].

—. 'Olson'. URL: <http://www.youtube.com/watch?v=2UYQqeLvHns> [last accessed 28 August 2012].

Leon Somov & Jazzu .'Sonnet'. URL: <http://www.youtube.com/watch?v=qtjPkKcMypE> [last accessed 28 August 2012].

Lusine. 'Baffle'. URL: <http://www.youtube.com/watch?v=xpJc28Wwj4s> [last accessed 28 August 2012].

—. 'Everything under the sun'. URL: <http://www.youtube.com/watch?v=sqQMndxLA0k> [last accessed 28 August 2012].

—. 'Gravity'. URL: <http://www.youtube.com/watch?v=l7smbG7myts&feature=related> (version current at 26 August 2012).

Matthew Dear. 'Headcage'. URL: <http://www.youtube.com/watch?v=CxCqeZESSkA> [last accessed 28 August 2012].

—. 'Juice'. URL: <http://www.youtube.com/watch?v=SSE4l2adiME> (version current at 27 August 2012).

Trentemoller. 'Forest'. URL: <http://www.youtube.com/watch?v=aij_LteJM8I> [last accessed 28 August 2012].

CHAPTER SEVEN

NON-CLASSICAL METHOD OF CLASSICAL MUSIC RECORDING

VYTAUTAS KEDERYS
KAUNAS UNIVERSITY OF TECHNOLOGY

This paper describes and compares two different methods of classical music recording. The first method is a classical method: all musicians are recorded together at once. The second method is unusual for classical music recording, because orchestra musicians are recorded separately, one after another. This project is a combination of research and practice, which presents the possibilities of a new method and compares it with the usual one. The orchestra recording was done using both of these methods and the final products are two different mixes.

The first aim was to research a new recording method and find out whether it is possible to achieve as good a result as when using the classical method. The second aim was to make a high fidelity, multichannel classical music recording with every instrument on an individual channel and fully isolated from each other. This recording was used for the interactive audiovisual installation "Virtual orchestra".

Virtual orchestra

The virtual orchestra is an interactive audiovisual installation where listeners can choose what instruments they want to hear during a music piece. Imagine a violinist who wants to have some more practice with the orchestra, but cannot because of the busy orchestra schedule. The "Virtual orchestra" would be a solution for this situation, because she or he could just mute the violin part, and by hearing the rest of the orchestra the violinist could play as well. Also, it could be used as an educational tool for music lessons as a presentation of the orchestra and of each instrument individually. This project required specific orchestra recording material: in order to have possibility of choosing any instrument you want to hear, you need to have each instrument on a separated channel and it should be perfectly isolated from other instruments. Thus if you select, for example, the bassoon on the installation and nothing else, you should hear only the bassoon without any other instruments. More information about the virtual orchestra can be found on the Internet: http://www.thevirtualorchestra.com.

Classical music recording history

The first known classical music recording was made by George Gouraud (foreign sales agent for Thomas Edison) on June 29, 1888 at the Crystal Palace, London. He recorded George Frideric Handel's *Israel in Egypt* using Edison's yellow paraffin cylinder. On a note with the cylinder was written: "A chorus of 4,000 voices recorded with phonograph over 100 yards away".[1] The conductor was Sir August Manns, conducting an orchestra of some 500 musicians and a choir of over 4,000 voices, in front of an audience of 23,722 people. These are the earliest deliberate recordings of music known to exist (earlier recordings from the 1870s are considered lost). Fortunately, these can be played back at a precise pitch, as we know the pitch of the Crystal Palace organ at this time.[2]

By the beginning of the 20th century, the music production industry was growing very fast, and music recording companies started to hire professional artists to record famous opera arias. One of the best known recording industry celebrities at that time was Enrico Caruso. Caruso became an exclusive artist for Victor Records. Caruso's first records were best sellers: he was, as Gaisberg later said, "the answer to the recording man's dream". He recorded well and his records sounded relatively rich when played on the primitive gramophones of the time. So popular were they that some of the masters wore out, and he had to re-record them in November of that year. This was before they were able to make multiple stampers from a single master.[3] Caruso's 1904 recording of *Vesti la giubba* was the first sound recording to sell a million copies.

The emergence of electrical recording technology was also a big improvement for the classical music recording industry. Electric recording techniques were able to capture a greater frequency range. Sound became more vivid and natural. As an example, listen to this recording from May 1926 of Chaliapin in a performance at Covent Garden.

Fig. 7-1: First known classical music recording – *Israel in Egypt*, London, 1888.

The next big step was probably magnetic tape recordings, which let engineers make stereo recordings. Although first invented in 1899, magnetic recording needed sophisticated electronics and a reliable medium. It was the Germans who really made it all work. When the Allies requisitioned German radio stations in 1945, tape recording was found to have advanced way beyond pre-war capabilities. Among the material recovered by the Russians were tape recordings in stereo, a few surviving examples of which resurfaced in the 1990s, including an astonishingly clear recording of Bruckner's 9th Symphony under Karajan recorded in Berlin in 1944. Compared to performances on contemporary 78rpm disc, it is truly remarkable.[3]

Finally, the music industry came of digital age with digital audio recordings. There were a few medium formats for digital audio, but CD (Compact Disc) became the most popular. Early in the summer of 1982, the first classical music CD was pressed in Langenhagen near Hannover, Germany, by the Polydor Pressing Operations plant. The disc contained a recording of Richard Strauss's *Eine Alpensinfonie* (in English, *An Alpine Symphony*), played by the Berlin Philharmonic and conducted by Herbert von Karajan.[4]

Orchestra: Württembergische Philharmonie Reutlingen

For the production, we collaborated with the Württembergische Philharmonie. Founded in 1945, the Württembergische Philharmonie has become an internationally recognized orchestra, and officially represents the state of Baden-Württemberg. Since the 2008/2009 season, Swedish conductor Ola Rudner has been Music Director of the Württembergische Philharmonie. Formerly artistic director, Japanese conductor Norichika Iimori continues his tenure as the orchestra's guest conductor.[5]

For this particular recording, we had an orchestra of 61 musicians: 12 first violins, 10 second violins, 8 violas, 6 cellos, 4 double basses, 2 flutes, 2 oboes, 2 clarinets, 2 bassoons, 4 horns, 3 trumpets, 3 trombones, 1 tuba, 1 percussion and 1 timpani.

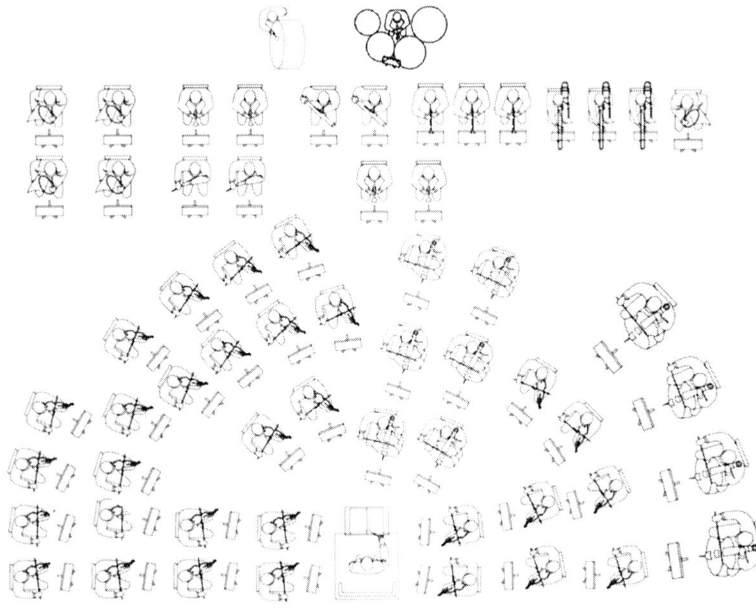

Fig. 7-2: Orchestra seating plan.

Musical composition

The requirements for choosing the piece were simple: the piece should not be longer than 15 minutes; otherwise it would take too much time to record, edit and mix it. Also, we were looking for a piece which should have as many parts as possible with all instruments being played at the same time so it would be easy to demonstrate our audiovisual installation. We did not expect the orchestra to learn a new piece, because it would just take extra time that neither the orchestra nor we had, thus we chose from the current season's repertoire. Finally, after some discussion, two pieces were left to choose between: 3rd movement - Presto – Assai meno presto (trio)) from Symphony No. 7 by Ludwig van Beethoven, and *Finlandia* Op. 26 composed by Jean Sibelius. Both pieces looked like a good choices, both are shorter than 10 minutes, both have parts where all the instruments play together (*Finlandia* has slightly more of this). In the end, after some discussion with conductor Ola Rudner, we decided to record *Finlandia*.

Recording method

The so-called "classical" or regular method of classical music recording, no matter if it is a studio recording or a concert recording, is when all the musicians play together. There is the main microphone system (room microphones) to record the whole picture and usually additional spot microphones for each instrument to record some more details.

The recording task for this project was to make a recording with perfectly isolated instruments. It meant that the regular recording method was not suitable because with the regular method, more or less every instrument could be heard on every channel. So it was necessary to come up with a different method.

One of the ideas was to use some acoustical walls and in this way, try to physically isolate instruments, but it would only help a little bit because you could still hear, for example, the percussion section on the first violin channels. Consequently there were two solutions: to record everything together but to have each instrument in a different room with a video of the conductor conducting for synchronization, or to record each instrument in the same room, but one after another, using audio and video of the full orchestra recorded together for reference. Both methods looked like a good solution. However, after some discussions and research, we decided to record the orchestra using the second method. The main reason for not choosing the first method was that it is very difficult to find fourteen rooms (we had fourteen groups of different instruments) in one building, which would be acoustically good enough to make recordings, and would have rather similar acoustical characteristics. The rooms could not be very small because our biggest group, the first violins, consisted of twelve musicians.

The method of recording instruments separately is not surprising in pop or rock music recording, but it is unusual for classical music. First of all, the players are used to playing together, surrounded by other instruments. Secondly, classical musicians are not used to playing with headphone reference, which in this situation was one of the solutions to the problem of how they could have the reference of the full orchestra recording. At a pop music recording session, the musicians usually use a metronome, but in our case we did not use this as the reference recording was supposed to take care of the metronome's function. Another interesting aspect of this method was seeing how musicians deal with this unusual situation, because while orchestral musicians are used to playing together as a group, in this situation each group of instruments acts like an individual soloist.

After deciding to record the musicians separately, I started thinking about the recording setup in the sense of microphone setup. Everything was clear about the first session, where the whole orchestra was playing together: some main pairs of microphones for a general picture and spot microphones for more instrument details. The question that came to my mind was how should I record instruments individually? Should I leave the whole system and record in the same way as with the classical method? Or should I think about going more individually? At this recording, I decided to use the same recording system for both recording methods. Firstly, to have the same recording setup so there would be a more equal comparison between the two methods. Secondly, I believe I will use this recording method in the future and I wanted to test everything; thus, this time, I decided to test with the same recording setup.

So all this led to an interesting work, with many questions: How will musicians deal with this situation? How will the conductor feel conducting with the reference of a previous recording? Is it possible to make a mix from individually recorded instruments? It is possible to make as good an orchestral recording using an unusual recording method as using a regular recording method?

Recording plan

One of the most important and biggest tasks was to make a recording plan and time schedule for the orchestra and for every instrument. To record instruments separately and to capture the same tempo, dynamics and emotions every time, we needed to use the full orchestra recording as a reference. So we had to start with the full orchestra recording. We were not sure how musicians would feel during recordings without a conductor.

But since we had only two days to make all the recordings, we had to work from early morning till evening, which would be physically too much for a conductor to conduct for all sessions. For this reason, we decided to record video as well as audio, to have both for reference – audio of all the orchestra playing, and video of the conductor conducting. The audio reference would be sent to headphones and the video would be shown on the wall using the projector. In the end, we had four possible ways of how we could make the recording:

1) Conductor listening to the full orchestra recording through headphones and conducting
2) Conductor and every musician with headphones
3) Conductor on the screen and every musician with headphones
4) No conductor, every musician with headphones

To make everything as clear and easy-going as possible, we discussed with the conductor about which solution would be the best, and finally we decided to do it like this: first to record the full orchestra, and then to start with the biggest instrument groups (first violins, second violins and violas. He suggested conducting for these groups, because he had some suspicions that these techniques would hardly work out with big groups of musicians and that it would be very difficult for musicians to play together without a conductor. We decided to make recording sessions in this sequential order: Full orchestra, Violin I, Violin II, Viola, Cello, Contrabass, Flute, Oboe, Clarinet, Bassoon, Horn, Trumpet, Trombone with Tuba, and last but not least, Percussion.

Editing

Editing was started with a new recording method session. The DAW project of the individual recording method consists of 50 channels (13 different instrument groups + AB pair for each group) and more than 200 takes. The editing process consisted of these steps:

1. The first step was to delete unnecessary material. For example, not all instruments started from the beginning, and some instruments had long pauses; thus I removed these sections in order to avoid any background noises which were recorded in the times when musicians were waiting to play their parts.

2. Looking for musically failed parts and replacing it with material from other takes. During recording, I took notes and marked on the scores the places in each take that was played correctly, or where there were problems, so this helped me a lot with finishing this task faster.

3. After choosing takes where the instruments were playing without mistakes, I tried to listen to some instruments together. For example, to listen to the first violin, then add the second violin, viola, cello and so on. Listening to the instruments together, I noticed rhythmic problems between instruments in some parts. Musicians, for example, might play some part of bar a little bit faster. So then I had to find a good take where the musicians played well and are in sync with other instruments. So this was quite a lot of work, and unfortunately there are some small parts where I didn't have a good take, so some small sync issues are audible.

4. The last step of editing was noise cleaning. For this task, the Samplitude Noise cleaning plugin was very useful.

Results

Two recordings were made using the classical method and the new recording method. Two different mixes have been finished. After recording and mixing, some results can be outlined. First of all, to compare these two methods, the new method takes more time to record. It saves the musicians' time, but extends the producer's work hours. Editing and mixing also takes more time with the new recording method. It's rather like 13 solo recordings aggregated into one recording, so you need to work on each instrument individually and then to merge all into one so that the final product sounds as if it is one full orchestra rather than individual instruments.

For a full comparison of the advantages and disadvantages of each recording method, see Table 7-1:

Table 7-1: comparison of recording methods

	Classical method	New method
Musician, conductor time	More. Musician can't rely only on himself; if other instruments make more mistakes, he needs to spend more time on recording. Conductor is needed for entire recording.	Less. Musicians can rely on their own playing level. Time depends only on how well he is playing. Conductor is not needed during entire recording.
Producer time	Less	More (in all phases: recording, editing and mixing)
Method complexity	Less complicated	More complicated. It requires reference (audio and/or video) and headphone monitoring.
Instrument separation	Instruments are separated poorly	Instruments are fully separated
Production cost		Cheaper if done in production line (more recordings on same day(s))
Musician convenience	Ordinary situation, musicians are used to play together	Less stress on recording (without conductor). Musician can focus more on his sound.
Tonal quality	Orchestra sounds natural	Sound engineer can focus more on an individual instrument, but the orchestra might not sound natural if musicians do not play identically rhythmically
Production schedule	All musicians are needed at the same time	Recordings do not need entire orchestra – easier to schedule just the groups of instruments

Conclusion

This method is especially suitable (or sometimes is the only method available) for particular tasks, as in this case where recording material was used for the audiovisual installation "Virtual orchestra", where all instruments must be fully separated.

To sum up, a new recording method has a good future, and to answer the main question of this paper, whether it is possible to reach as good a result as using the classical method, it is clear that the answer is yes, affirmative: with some improvements, high quality recordings can be done (listen to CD-ROM music files 11 and 12).

Notes

[1] Very early recorded sounds http://www.nps.gov/edis/photosmultimedia/very-early-recorded-sound.htm [last accessed 7 November 2013]
[2] Orchestra biography http://www.wuerttembergische-philharmonie.de/ [last accessed 2 December 2012]
[3] History of recorded music http://www.charm.rhul.ac.uk/history/ [last accessed 2 December 2012]
[4] Compact Disc history http://en.wikipedia.org/wiki/Compact_Disc [last accessed 4 December 2012]
[5] *Musica. 1000 Years of Classical Music.* 2010. Elanora Heights: Millennium House. EISBN 978-1-921209-76-5.

CHAPTER EIGHT

THE RÔLE OF SOUND RECORDING IN BLURRING THE LINE OF DISTINCTION BETWEEN MUSIC AND NOISE: THE CASE OF SOUNDSCAPE

ANTANAS KUČINSKAS
LITHUANIAN ACADEMY OF MUSIC AND THEATRE

Music and technology go hand in hand, all of the time. If music technology can be defined as any form of technology helping to make, transmit or consume music (from acoustic musical instruments to samplers, synthesizers and computer technology), so the impact of technology on music is overwhelming. New music ideas require new technological equipment; new technologies inspire new artistic ideas. This correlation is mutual and reversible. The question 'which is first?' is the same as the question 'which came first: the chicken or the egg?' Did the decline of the modal harmony system in the late Renaissance and the emergence of the tonal system in Baroque bring the equally tempered tuning system to life? Or did the making of the 'well-tempered' keyboard allow J. S. Bach to compose preludes and fugues for all possible tonalities? Both statements are right.

In the second part of the 19th century, the sound recording device was invented. The rapid evolution of sound recording equipment (from phonographs and gramophones, to tape recorders and digital recording systems) radically changed the way we make, listen to, and market music, as well as changing the fundamental understanding of what we call music. Some authors propose that the possibility of acoustic recording restored archaic musical thinking, which was principally aural and which was then supplanted by a written (visual) tradition for many centuries (Eisenberg 2005). Now is not necessary for a composer to use notation or scores to transfer music to listeners. The audio fixation is much more precise and unlimited than any visual representation. It brings music directly without any visual intermediate. Finally, any sound with the help of recording gained the musical feature of being reproduced, controlled and synchronized with the sounds of musical instruments. But that process was not so straightforward.

In the 19th century, the famous German psychoacoustician Hermann Helmholtz stated: 'the first and principal difference between various sounds experienced by our ear, is that between noises and musical sounds' (Helmholtz 1862). The criteria to distinguish between sounds thus were mainly physical – musical sounds produce the sound of periodic waves, so-called tones, as well as noises; non-periodic waves are interpreted as random. But if we look at the history of 20th-century music, we can see a very clear shifting to 'music out of tone', to music which from the point of view of Helmholtz would be noise – the experiments of the futurists, the music of E. Varèse and J. Cage, Fluxus and other movements of conceptual art, examples of concrete, sonoristic (sound mass), electronic music and so on. The same applies if we go back to archaic ethno-music or look at a variety of non-European musical traditions – African or Japanese drumming, and Tibetan, Indonesian, Australian Aboriginal music, and so forth. It is obvious that the physical criteria to distinguish between music and noise are too narrow. The majority of contemporary observers find socio-cultural criteria as an essential to qualify sound objects as music. The forming of those criteria seems to be closely related to the evolution of music carriers, i.e. music technologies. In the acoustic music era, any soundscape ('noise') had to be adapted to the possibilities of musical instruments and imitated by them in order to be fixed and carried to listeners. Subjective and socio-cultural 'filters' changed the sounding of natural sounds very radically and differently. So this type of relationship between soundscape and music could be defined as imitative.

Aspirations to move away from imitative methods of working with soundscapes and towards more productive manufacturing tools are seen already in the first decades of the 20th century, especially in the experiments of one of the leaders of Italian futurism, Lugi Russolo. If for Hermann Helmholtz it was quite clear that the soughing, howling, and whistling of the wind, the splashing of the water, and the rolling of carriages, are examples of noise (meaning not musical), thus sounds, for Luigi Russolo, became much more musical than the boring music of fixed pitches, of tones. In his 1913 publication 'L'arte dei rumori', Russolo announced: 'We must break at all cost from this restrictive circle of pure sounds and conquer the infinite variety of noise-sounds' (Russolo 1913, 6). And he did it by producing a whole array of 'noise-making' instruments – *Intonarumoriums* – which played different mechanically and electrically produced sounds, the 'examples' of a future urban soundscape.

The development of sound recording devices gave new impulses for capturing already existing environmental sounds and using them for art purposes. 'Although it was already possible to record sound in Russolo's times, and although with traditional vinyl it was already possible to manipulate sound (loops, cutting off the attack), it was only the introduction of the tape that made it possible to produce all kinds of sounds in a more economic way than building futuristic instruments' (Beyst 2004).

In 1930 the German filmmaker Walter Ruttmann (1887-1941) created an experimental film, 12 minutes in duration, with only sound and no image, which he titled *Wochenende* (Weekend). It is a sound collage made from short sound recordings in Berlin, 'the story of [a] weekend, from the moment the trains leaves the city until the whispering lovers are separated by the approaching, home-struggling crowd. It was a symphony of sound, speech-fragments and silence woven into a poem' (Cory 1992). The objectivity of recorded sounds and the subjectivity of selection and montage generated a strange result which could be comparable with the case of photography. That 'blind film' anticipated by more than a decade the well-known concrete music by Pierre Schaeffer, composed only from cuts of environmental sound recordings and played on the radio.

The potential possibilities of radio media for sound art were understood and explored before Pierre Schaeffer's first public 'concerts'. The colleague and follower of Russolo, Filippo Tommaso Marinetti, took a conceptual approach in one of his Futurist Wireless Syntheses, created between 1927 and 1938. His *Un paesaggio udito* (A heard landscape) suggested the juxtaposition of sounds captured in different physical spaces and circumstances which the radio adapted to its electronic space, in order to compose a reality of its own.[1]

Closely related ideas also took possession of the composer John Cage. His *Imaginary Landscapes* (1939-1952)[2] could be given as another good example of a designed soundscape. This composition used different recorded or played noises as radio, and other sound equipment sounds as well. So when in 1948 the French composer Pierre Schaeffer began to demonstrate concrete music compositions – audio collages made from recordings of different environmental sounds – it was rather a culmination than a beginning of noise music which required a new acousmatic listening experience: listening 'without referring to seeing the causes behind it' (Schaeffer 1966, 91). And one of the main preconditions of that was the invention and development of sound recording.

In all above mentioned cases – from Russolo to Cage – the design lies in essence in turning soundscape (noise) into music, but it still provides a platform for the individuality of the composer. Understanding that, and influenced by ideas from Zen Buddhism, John Cage became more and more interested in silence. The culmination of that was his famous silent composition *4'33'* (1952). The piece purports to consist of the sounds of the environment that listeners hear while it is 'performed', i.e. not performed. That conceptual work very clear showed that silence as such does not exist, and that changing the point of listening herewith changes the quality of the soundscape, bringing it from 'shadow noise' to 'music surface'.

These ideas of active listening were captured and exploited by Canadian musician and researcher R. Murray Schafer for acoustic ecology[3] purposes. The most significant international research project founded by him was the 'World soundscape project' started in the late 1960s. Its ultimate goal was to find solutions for an ecologically balanced soundscape where the relationship between the human community and its sonic environment is one of harmony. If Pierre Schaeffer dignifies sound objects – what we are interested in here are those of the natural and urban acoustic environment – as elements of a composition, then R. Murray Schafer gives them an ethical dimension (Beyst 2004). Founding, documenting and preserving the acoustic environment in R. Murray Schafer's practice pushed aside the desires of collecting and transforming noises which were seen by previous inventors or current developers of noise and of electroacoustic music (Halim El-Dabh, James Tenney, Karlheinz Stockhausen, Pauline Oliveros and others). Studying soundscapes, R. M. Schafer introduced special parameters and terms such as sound mark, key sound, low-fi, hi-fi, and schizophonia, etc. Although some of them were projections of musical terms, it helped to establish an independent vocabulary and the principles of soundscape studies. Finally R. M. Schafer's considerations and studies of the sound environment gave an impulse to a wide movement of acoustic ecology. And portable sound recording devices of course were a primary and inseparable part of the equipment of soundscape researchers.

The prevalence of recording devices in everyday life allowed not only professionals to be engaged in soundscape inventions. It enlarged the forms of soundscape research and application. A lot of CD releases, internet radios, and data banks specialized in environmental sounds, as well as open source sound maps, arose in ascending progression.[4] As photography emerged as a creative medium a century ago, soundscape art is coming alive as an emerging experimental art. Separate directions of soundscape art could now be defined by such styles as purist documentaries ('what you hear, what you get'), reconstructions (many source recordings are combined in the creation of a single soundscape experience), transformations (the use of field recordings as the raw material for electronic transformations and manipulations) and finally musical compositions (adding human instruments or voices to the mix) (Cummings).[5]

Summarizing all that has been mentioned above, we have to emphasize once more the bi-directional interaction between the evolution of sound recording technologies and noise becoming music. If we follow the evolution of sound recording equipment, we see that the invention of audio recording directly stimulated the process of including environmental sounds into the vocabulary of contemporary music. On the other hand, it also created new conditions to listen to and investigate the soundscape. In the era of acoustic musical instruments, only the soundscape imitated by music instruments became music. In the 20th century's modernistic attitude, soundscapes (noise) recorded and montaged in a composition became music. From a postmodern view, any soundscape – recorded and listened to, or simply heard – equates to music. That curve of noise transformation to music could be compared with the broadening of sound recording technologies and other music technologies in our everyday life. With the help of sound recording, the soundscape was again heard and gained its own musical worth. Conversely, traditional instrumental or vocal music lost hegemony, becoming only one among several manifestations of music.

Notes

[1] Marinetti's text, reminiscent of the spirit of the haiku, reads as follows:

A LANDSCAPE HEARD

The whistling of the blackbird jealous of the crackling of the fire ends up silencing the murmur of the water.

10 seconds of splashing
1 second of crackling
8 seconds of splashing
1 second of crackling
5 seconds of splashing
1 second of crackling
19 seconds of splashing
1 second of crackling
25 seconds of splashing
1 second of crackling
35 seconds of splashing
6 seconds of blackbird whistling
(Collected in Sarmiento 1993).

[2] *Imaginary Landscape No. 1* (1939) – two variable-speed turntables, frequency recordings, muted piano, and cymbal; *Imaginary Landscape No. 2 (March)* (1942) – tin cans, conch shell, ratchet, bass drum, buzzers, water gong, metal wastebasket, lion's roar and amplified coil of wire; *Imaginary Landscape No. 3* (1942) – tin cans, muted gongs, audio frequency oscillators, variable speed turntables with frequency recordings and recordings of generator whines, amplified coil of wire, amplified marimbula (a Caribbean instrument similar to the African thumb piano), and electric buzzer; *Imaginary Landscape No. 4 (March No. 2)* (1951) – 24 performers at 12 radios; *Imaginary Landscape No. 5* (1952) – magnetic tape recording of any of 42 phonograph records.
[3] Acoustic ecology – is the study of the effects of the acoustic environment or *soundscape* on the physical responses or behavioral characteristics of creatures living within it. Its particular aim is to draw attention to imbalances which may have unhealthy or inimical effects.
[4] Some of them: Aporee radio and global sound map project www.aporee.org, project "Sounds of Europe" www.soundsofeurope.eu, London "Sound Survey Project" www.soundsurvey.org.uk, New York "Sound Seeker Project" www.soundseeker.org, international programme "Listen to the Deep Ocean" (LIDO) www.listentothedeep.com and many others created using Google Maps or Google Earth, internet sound banks www.freesound.org, www.findsounds.com, examples of Lithuanian soundscapes www.soundscape.lt, etc.
[5] Some of wider known soundscape artists and works: Francisco López (a large amount of sound pieces with record labels from more than fifty countries); Bill

Fontana, "Sound bridge Köln-San Francisco" (1987) and "Landscape Soundings" (1990); Mario Gauthier; Claire Bourque, "7th Electro-Acoustic Spring" (1992); Gerhard Rühm, "*Wien wie es klingt*" (Vienna as it sounds, 1991-1992), and others.

References

Beyst, Stefan. *Three types of soundscape, one music*... http://d-sites.net/english/soundscape.htm [last accessed 12 September 2013].

Cory, Mark E. 1992. *Wireless Imagination: Sound, Radio, and the Avant-Garde*. Cambridge, MA: MIT Press.

Cummings, Jim. *Styles of Environmental Sound Compositions*. http://greenmuseum.org/c/vop/vop_styles.php [last accessed 12 September 2013].

Eisenberg, Evan. 2005. *The Recording Angel: Music, Records and Culture from Aristotle to Zappa*. Yale University Press.

Hegarty, Paul. 2007. *Noise music: a History*. New York: Continuum.

Helmholtz, Hermann. 2005. *On the Sensations of Tone as a Physiological Basis for the Theory of Music*. 1862, reprinted Kessinger Publishing.

Iges, José. *Soundscapes: a Historical Approach*. http://cec.sonus.ca/econtact/Histories/HistoricalApproach.htm [last accessed 20 September 2013].

Ross, Alex. 2011. *The Rest Is Noise: Listening to the Twentieth Century*. Harper Collins Publishers.

Russolo, Luigi. The Art of Noise (1913). In Christoph Cox, Daniel Warner. 2004. *Audio Culture– Readings in Modern Music*. New York: Continuum, p. 10-14.

Sarmiento, José Antonio. 1993. *Marinetti: La radio futurista*. Cuenca: Radio Fontana Mix.

Schaeffer, Pierre. 1966. *Traité des objets musicaux*. Paris: Le Seuil.

Schaffer, Ray Murray. 1977. *The Tuning of the World*. New York: Knopf.

Truax, Barry. 2001. *Acoustic communication*. Greenwood Publishing Group.

Voegelin, Salomé. 2010. *Listening to Noise and Silence: Towards a Philosophy of Sound Art*. New York: Continuum.

Chapter Nine

Investigating the Perception of Structural Boundaries in Steve Reich's *City Life*

Nerdinga Letulė, Duncan L. Snape and Marc R. Thompson
University of Jyväskylä

Introduction

Researchers have argued that the scale of our daily exposure to music represents an 'informal learning environment' (ILE), from which we develop both familiarity with music and individual preferences (Batt-Rawden & De Nora 2005). When we consider this idea, it is not to be wondered at that the differences between non-musicians (informal learners) and musicians (formal learners) have been found to be relatively small in a variety of tasks related to the perception of music (Bigand & Poulin-Charonnat 2006). Each individual's informal training begins before birth (Granier-Deferre & Busnel 2013) and there is evidence that 'there is an initial predisposition of the human brain for music processing that is triggered by the extensive exposition to musical stimuli in everyday life.' (Bigand & Poulin-Charonnat 2006, 120).

The perception of music relies on the segmentation of the auditory stream into smaller units, melodic phrases and motifs. On the surface, this segmentation would seem to be quite subjective and arbitrary, and yet in the compositional styles of many musical eras and genres, clear structural rules that listeners, both informally and formally trained, can become familiar with, exist. The sonata and rondo forms from the art music of the late 18th and 19th centuries (Cadwallader & Gagne 2010), and the variations around the structure of ABABCAB in popular songs (Cooper &

Foote, 2003), are some examples of these. It is reasonable, therefore, to suppose that, due to repeated exposure to music in the ILE that obeys these structural rules, any individual might become familiar with common structural forms from a relatively early age without formal training. If we seek to understand how the structural perception of music occurs in individuals, it follows that we need to present participants with musical stimuli that circumvent their familiarity and require the full engagement of cognitive processes.

Studies focusing on the investigation of structure in music have employed a variety of methods in analysing both stimuli and results. The most common of these come from two quite distinct areas of research – musicological analysis and music information retrieval (MIR). The musicological approach is based on the extraction and interpretation of musical features from score notation (Cadwallader & Gagne 2010; Beach 2012). Examples of this include Schenkerian analysis and the Generative Theory of Tonal Music (Lerdahl & Jackendorf 1983). Computational systems perform music feature analysis on digital musical data, either audio or MIDI. One of the most commonly applied methods in the assessment of structure is that of self-similarity. The acoustic similarity between any two instances of an audio recording is displayed as a two-dimensional comparative figure (Foote 1999). The output of the self-similarity matrix can be further processed by finding repeated patterns and points of novelty (Cooper & Foote 2003).

Research Aims

The following study aimed to explore the perception of structural boundaries amongst both informally and formally trained listeners, in a piece of music that did not conform to commonly-experienced structural rules. It also sought to compare the results of a musicological analysis to those of a computational analysis with regard to which better represented the results of listener perceptions. With these aims in place, an experiment was conducted to investigate the following questions:

- Is there consensus as to the salience and temporal point of the structural boundary?
- Do participants with and without formal musical training perceive structural boundaries differently?
- Which analysis method (musicological or computational) more closely approximates listener perceptions?

Previous Studies

There have been a number of previous studies that have compared the perception of musical structure of informally trained (IT) and formally trained (FT) participants, although these labels are only applied in this study. Some of these have used stimuli from within the ILE, others from outside it.

Starting with those studies that worked within the ILE, Deliège (1987) used material from recordings of Bach, Mozart, Beethoven and Stravinsky and found very little difference in segmentation patterns between IT and FT participants. The difference that was observed was that FT participants tended to place fewer boundaries and group items into longer segments. Krumhansl (1996) used Mozart's Piano Sonata K. 282 and found that the groups showed broad consensus on structural changes. Bruderer, McKinney & Kohlrausch (2009) used a number of popular songs by Billie Holliday, Paul McCartney, and Van Morrison amongst others. They found that there was considerable variety in the number and location of boundaries identified between participants. This was significantly linked to the salience of changes in the stimuli, but their results showed no significant effect as a result of formal training. The results of these studies are not unexpected, given that we presuppose both groups of participants to have had similar levels of exposure, through the ILE, to the underlying rules of structure governing the music used as stimuli.

Deliège & Ahmadi (1990), on the other hand, presented their participants with music from outside the ILE, from post-tonal composer Luciano Berio. Nevertheless, they still found that there was general agreement between the responses of both groups and those of two experts. Addessi & Caterina asked their participants to segment the music of Bruno Maderna (2002) and Kurtág (2005), and in both cases found very little evidence of an influence of formal training on results. These results are, perhaps, a little more surprising. In a situation where participants are presented with material that does not follow expected rules, we might expect a FT participant to have more preparation for the successful identification of a structural boundary than an IT participant. However, it can equally be argued that the extra preparation a FT participant receives might relate only to the repertoire of one instrument, style or era.

Finally, with regard to the question of comparison of different analysis methods, we were able to find relatively few studies. The one considered most relevant to the current study was Leman et al. (2005), where manual (score) and acoustical (computed) structural cues were used to predict the musical affect of participants. Their results showed that manual cues were more successful than acoustical.

Experimental Methodology

Particular consideration was given in the design of the following to both external and ecological validity. It was reasoned that in order to achieve the capture of those cognitive processes involved in the everyday perception of music, we should undertake to capture them under circumstances approximating everyday conditions. Data would be gathered in as naturalistic a setting as possible, following the recommendations of Brewer (2000). This reasoning had a considerable impact on the design of experimental instruments, the location and approach of data gathering, and choice of stimuli.

In both experiments a portable experimental setup consisting of a laptop and high quality closed-back headphones was used. Participants were recruited opportunistically and data was gathered in public areas where it was expected participants would be likely to be listening to music naturally. The combined excerpt player and data gather tool, created in Max MSP (v6.0) and used in both the reaction time test and perception experiment, was designed to look and function like a contemporary media or MP3 player, so that participants would feel comfortable and familiar with the interface. A pilot study with exit survey (N = 6) of the perception experiment was also conducted in order to improve both the instructions and presentation to participants.

City Life was decided on as the source of stimuli in order to present participants with musical excerpts that did not follow structural rules that were expected from the ILE. Where the approach differed from other studies was in the desire to present participants with unfamiliar structural boundaries, whilst maintaining familiar harmonic content. If we consider the works of Maderna, Berio or Kurtág featured in those other studies, all three present a dense and relatively inaccessible post-tonal approach, combining rhythmic irregularity, stark instrumentation and strictly atonal or dissonant harmonics. *City Life*, by contrast, is both melodic and harmonic in a more traditional way. It represented a controlled departure from the ILE along desirable lines.

Reaction Time Test

The aim of the reaction time test was to establish a window of reaction time that could be linked to specific musical events in the stimuli in the perception experiment. Reaction times were captured using the experimental setup already discussed. A random sample of opportunistically recruited participants (N = 50) completed the test. The stimulus was a 10-second audio file, in which the notes of a major third interval, created using an artificial sound source, were introduced sequentially. Participants were asked to press a button when they perceived the onset of the second note of the dyad. They were given the opportunity to press as many times as they wished to position their response as near to the note onset as they felt was appropriate.

Responses varied from 223 ms to 997 ms, with a mean of 488 ms. Based on these results it was decided to allow a 1000 ms window of response after the onset of an event in the stimuli, into which responses could be clustered.

Perception Experiment: Method

Two groups of 10 opportunistically recruited participants (N = 20) took part: those with informal training (IT), and those with formal training (FT). FT participants were recruited from among the students and faculty of the Music Department at the University of Jyväskylä, and IT participants were a random sample recruited in the main library of the University. Three 20-second excerpts were selected from *City Life* as stimuli, with the goal of presenting structural boundaries with decreasing salience.

Excerpts were evaluated and selected based on a method of score analysis devised with the aim of making identified structural changes more easily comparable to audio analysis. This analysis was linked to feature changes. Four defined features – Dynamics, Harmony, Tempo, and Timbre – which had been linked to specific computational analysis functions, were used, plus one undefined feature – Other. Other was used for any other notated cue of structural boundary (e.g. rhythmic change, pause, textural change, repetition). Each feature was considered to have equal importance. These features were analysed in the score in order to determine the point of the greatest number of simultaneous feature changes in each excerpt, which, it was reasoned, would signify the point of a structural boundary. Using this method the most significant point of change (MSP) and the salience of change (SoC) rating, equal to the number of features that changed at that point, were identified.

Audio analysis was performed on the excerpts using the MIR Toolbox (v1.4) functions in Matlab (R2012a). Peaks were highlighted on a novelty curve extracted from a self-similarity matrix, which was based on a time-decomposed spectrogram. This series of functions accounted in some measure for four of the features used in the musicological approach – Dynamics, Harmony, Timbre and Other (Rhythm). Because novelty curves are measured against a coefficient value of relative novelty, a novelty peak, the point of greatest relative novelty (PGN) in each excerpt, was also identified.

Participants were asked to listen to each excerpt and decide if there was a significant change. If they could identify more than one change, then they were instructed to choose the one they considered the strongest. Participants were asked to press a button on the keyboard when this change occurred. Again, they were able to press the button as many times as they wanted. They were then asked to rate the salience of the change on a Likert-type scale from 1 to 5, where 5 corresponded to the greatest salience. Participants were able to leave all options blank and move to the next clip if they felt that there was no change in an excerpt. Excerpts were presented to each participant in random order (listen to CD-ROM sound files 13, 14, 15).

Perception Experiment: Results

Excerpt 1

Score analysis revealed that the MSP in this excerpt occurred on the first beat of bar 25. This point was at 9325 ms in the audio. The boundary salience was rated four, as at this point four features – Harmony, Dynamics, Timbre, Other (Rhythm) – changed simultaneously. Computational analysis showed that the PGN was at 6875 ms.

Figure 1 shows the temporal location of the responses of both groups of participants, plotted against salience ratings. Responses were linked to events using the 1000 ms window established in Experiment 1.

The majority of participant responses could be linked to three events. Event A is the PGN. It is the onset of the chord at bar 23 in the score, which is preceded by a quarter note rest. Event B is the MSP. At this point there is an ambiguity (Wagner, 1995): a chord from the previous bar is held for an eighth note into bar 25, overlapping the MSP. This creates uncertainty as to whether the new section starts with the MSP (Bi) or the end of the chord (Bii). We allowed a further window of 300ms (the length of the overlap), as well as the established 1000 ms, to account for this uncertainty. Event C is the introduction of a recorded sample 'Check it out', at bar 30 (15875 ms). Two participant responses could not be linked to events or to any other responses (see Figure 9-1).

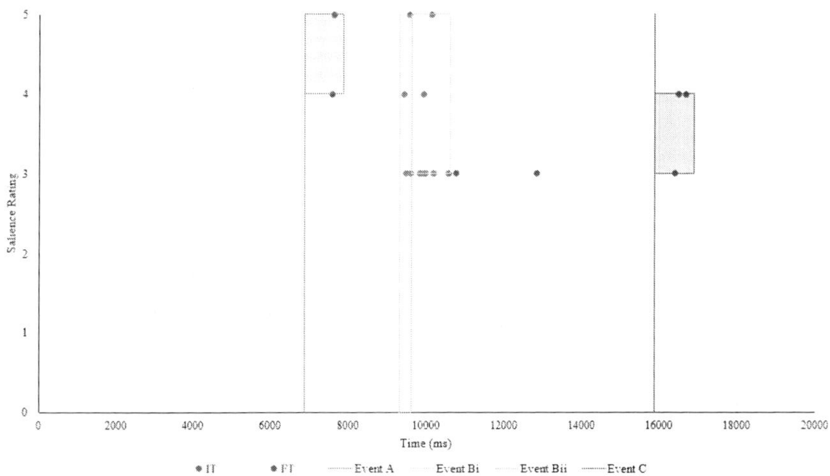

Fig. 9-1: Temporal responses of both groups of participants to excerpt 1, plotted against the salience rating.

Excerpt 2

Analysis of the score revealed that the MSP in this excerpt occurred on the second beat of bar 499. This was at 12275 ms in the audio. The boundary salience was rated three, as at this point three features (Harmony, Timbre, Other (Texture)) changed simultaneously. Computational analysis showed that the PGN was at 8125 ms.

The majority of participant responses could be linked to two events: A and D (Fig. 3). Event A is the onset of the note on the first beat of bar 496 in the score, played on clarinet and violin (5775 ms) (ten responses). Event D is the onset of the note on the first beat of bar 502 in the score, played on clarinet and violin (17425 ms) (five responses). No participants responded to the PGN (Event B on the graph) or the MSP (Event C). Five participants responded in other ways. Four participant responses could not be linked to events in the score or to any other responses, and one further participant (represented at point (0,0) on the graph) identified that there was no change in the excerpt (see Figure 9-2).

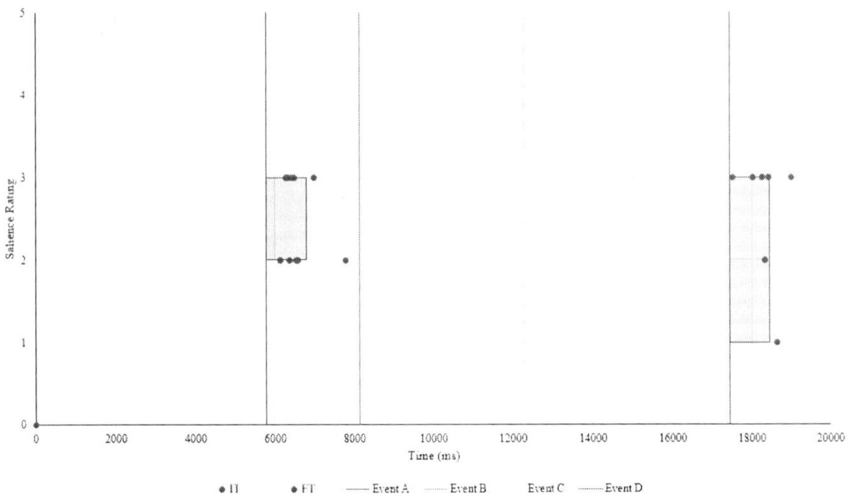

Fig. 9-2: Temporal responses of both groups of participants to excerpt 2, plotted against the salience rating.

Excerpt 3

The MSP for this excerpt was rated as No Change. Analysis of the score revealed that this excerpt comprised a series of repetitions (Ockleford, 2005). The initial event occurred on the first beat of bar 709 in the score (125 ms). This was repeated four times; at bar 715 (4925 ms), 722 (10325 ms), 728 (15125 ms), and 733 (19025 ms). This created a number of two (Harmony, Timbre or Harmony, Other (Rhythm)) feature changes with no point emerging as more salient than another. Audio analysis showed that the PGN was at 15125 ms (bar 728).

The largest group of participant responses were those who identified that there was no change in the excerpt (represented at point (0,0) on the graph (Fig. 5)). The greater part of the remaining responses could be linked to three events. Event A is the introduction of a recorded sample 'stand by stand by' at bar 716 (5725 ms). Event B is the onset of the chord on the first beat of bar 722. At this point there is a variation in the repetition – the start of the sustained chord is staggered over two beats, each marked with a separate drum hit. Event C is the PGN. Four participant responses could not be linked to events or to other responses (see Figure 9-3).

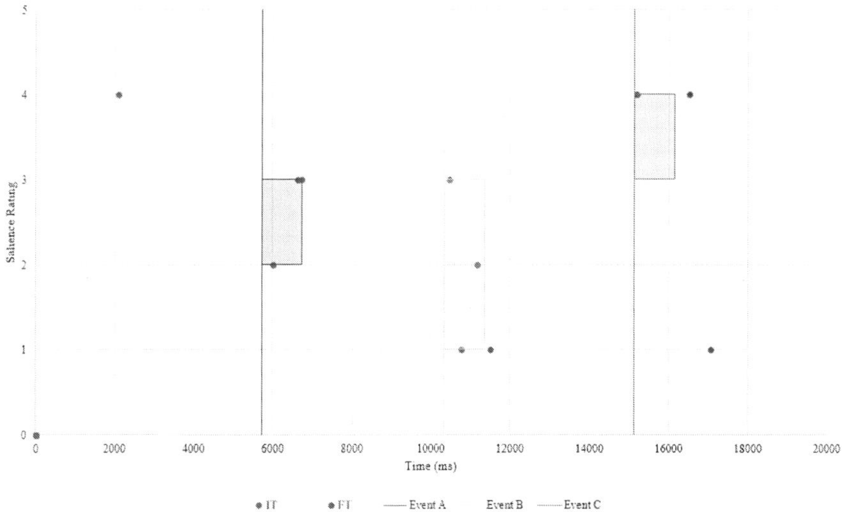

Fig. 9-3: Temporal responses of both groups of participants to excerpt 3, plotted against the salience rating.

Overall Results

On the question of consensus, it was found that there was a perfect negative correlation between the salience rating of structural boundaries in the excerpts and the number of distinct responses of participants as to the temporal location and salience of the structural boundary ($r = -1$ $p = .00$).

There were clear differences between the responses of the two participant groups. IT participants showed significantly more consensus on the point of the structural boundary (M = 2.67, SD = 1.53) than FT participants (M = 5.67, SD = 0.58), t (4) = -3.18, $p < .05$, and showed more consensus on the salience of the structural boundary (M = 3.00, SD = 1.73) than FT participants (M = 3.67, SD = 0.57), t (4) = -0.63, p = .56. Whilst only the former finding was significant, the latter observably followed the same general trend, with the mean number of distinct responses for IT participants lower than that of FT participants.

Using chi-square tests of goodness-of-fit, it was determined that IT participants were significantly less likely to choose the PGN when deciding on the temporal location of the structural boundary, x^2 (2, N = 30) = 15, p = .00. They were also more likely than FT participants to choose the MSP as the temporal location of the structural boundary. Whilst a further chi-square test of goodness-of-fit did not reveal a significant result, x^2 (1, N = 22) = 2.22, p = .13, it was again observed that 15 (half of the overall number) IT responses were linked to the MSP, compared to 7 (less than one quarter of) FT responses.

FT participants were significantly more likely to choose neither the MSP nor the PGN, x^2 (2, N = 30) = 15.8, p = .00, when temporally locating the structural boundary. They were more likely than IT participants to choose the salience rating identified by score analysis, x^2 (1, N = 26) = 0.04, p = .84, although the difference on the last point was very small.

A final chi-square test of goodness-of-fit revealed that, overall, participants were significantly less likely to choose the PGN when temporally locating the structural boundary, x^2 (2, N = 60) = 25.9, p = .00.

Discussion

The findings of this study broadly fall into two parts. The expected result was embodied in the finding that if structural boundaries were more salient, so participants' responses exhibited more consensus and less variation, in line with the findings of Bruderer, McKinney & Kohlrausch (2009).

The unexpected finding was the amount and nature of the variation between the participant groups. In the early stages of this experiment, it was expected that there would either be no difference between groups, as found by previous studies, or that FT participants might perform better at the task. Instead the study found the exact opposite. IT participants showed more consensus in both aspects of the experiment, and were more likely to choose the structural boundary identified by score analysis than their FT counterparts. These findings would support those of Bigand & Poulin-Charronnat (2006), that one does not need formal training to become an 'experienced listener'.

Questions remain, however, as to why the variation between participant groups was so pronounced. Further research would need to use a larger and wider sample in order to fully account for this. There is the possibility that the variation is due to some identified methodological limitations. The version of musicological analysis employed in this study was necessarily limited in order to define a simple method of equating musicological and computational analysis. The selection of only five features, four defined and one undefined, would inevitably impact on the level of analysis possible. The term *structural boundary* was replaced with *most significant point of feature change* in the instructions to participants, on the assumption that the two were commensurate, in line with the reasoning of Addessi & Caterina (2002). This was not always the case, as exemplified by the results of Excerpt 2, where no participants perceived a boundary at either point generated by the analysis methods. Further research is required to test the robustness of these approaches in evaluating other pieces of music.

Finally, it was necessary to use computational feature extraction in order to acquire temporal points that reaction windows could be linked to. This proved problematic since the computational system used relied heavily on single feature analysis, and human perception (and musicological analysis) does not. The series of functions used provided the nearest approximation, in our estimation, to a perceptual approach, basing computations on analysis of a spectrogram which could account for a wider range of features, particularly when time-decomposed. The limitation of such a system was that, as identified by Leman et al. (2005), the extracted points still needed to be related to musical features using musicological analysis. Also, as was evident in the differences between the MSP, the PGN, and the relative number of responses linked to each, our findings further supported those of Leman at al. in that 'manual structural cues worked better than acoustical structural cues.' (Leman et al. 2005, 59).

Summary and Conclusions

We have presented experimental data on how participants segmented excerpts and linked that data to musicological and audio analysis. Our results are applicable to musicology, music psychology and music information retrieval, because they show some of the ways in which perception of non-traditionally structured music differs between participant groups, and from the results of theoretical approaches.

We found that when structural boundaries were more salient, participants' responses exhibited more consensus and less variation. Informally trained participants showed more overall consensus and were more likely to choose the temporal location of the structural boundary identified by score analysis. Participants overall were less likely to choose the temporal location of the structural boundary identified by computational analysis.

References

Anna R. Addessi & Roberto Caterina, 2002. Perception of the macroform in the Quartetto per Archi in due tempi (1955) by Bruno Maderna. *Second International Conference: Understanding and Creating Music.* Caserta, Seconda Università degli Studi di Napoli.

—. 2005. Analysis and perception in post-tonal music: an example from Kurtág's String Quartet Op. 1. *Psychology of Music*, 33 (1), 94-116.

Kari Batt-Rawden & Tia DeNora, 2005. Music and informal learning in everyday life. *Music Education Research*, 7(3), 289-304.

David Beach, 2012. *Advances Schenkerian Analysis: Perspectives on Phrase Rhythm, Motive, and Form.* New York: Routledge.

Emmanuel Bigand & Bénédicte Poulin-Charronnat, 2006. Are we "experienced listeners"? A review of the musical capacities that do not depend on formal musical training. *Cognition*, 100(1), 100-130.

Michael J. Bruderer, Martin F. Mckinney & Armin Kohlrausch, 2009. The perception of structural boundaries in melody lines of Western popular music. *Musicae Scientiae*, 8(2), 273-313.

Alan C. Cadwallader, David Gagne & Alan Cadwallader, 1998. *Analysis of Tonal Music: A Schenkerian Approach.* Oxford: Oxford University Press.

Matthew Cooper & Jonathan Foote, 2003. Summarising Popular Music via Structural Similarity Analysis. *Proceedings of IEEE Workshop on*

Summary and Conclusions

We have presented experimental data on how participants segmented excerpts and linked that data to musicological and audio analysis. Our results are applicable to musicology, music psychology and music information retrieval, because they show some of the ways in which perception of non-traditionally structured music differs between participant groups, and from the results of theoretical approaches.

We found that when structural boundaries were more salient, participants' responses exhibited more consensus and less variation. Informally trained participants showed more overall consensus and were more likely to choose the temporal location of the structural boundary identified by score analysis. Participants overall were less likely to choose the temporal location of the structural boundary identified by computational analysis.

References

Anna R. Addessi & Roberto Caterina, 2002. Perception of the macroform in the Quartetto per Archi in due tempi (1955) by Bruno Maderna. *Second International Conference: Understanding and Creating Music*. Caserta, Seconda Università degli Studi di Napoli.

—. 2005. Analysis and perception in post-tonal music: an example from Kurtág's String Quartet Op. 1. *Psychology of Music*, 33 (1), 94-116.

Kari Batt-Rawden & Tia DeNora, 2005. Music and informal learning in everyday life. *Music Education Research*, 7(3), 289-304.

David Beach, 2012. *Advances Schenkerian Analysis: Perspectives on Phrase Rhythm, Motive, and Form*. New York: Routledge.

Emmanuel Bigand & Bénédicte Poulin-Charronnat, 2006. Are we "experienced listeners"? A review of the musical capacities that do not depend on formal musical training. *Cognition*, 100(1), 100-130.

Michael J. Bruderer, Martin F. Mckinney & Armin Kohlrausch, 2009. The perception of structural boundaries in melody lines of Western popular music. *Musicae Scientiae*, 8(2), 273-313.

Alan C. Cadwallader, David Gagne & Alan Cadwallader, 1998. *Analysis of Tonal Music: A Schenkerian Approach*. Oxford: Oxford University Press.

Matthew Cooper & Jonathan Foote, 2003. Summarising Popular Music via Structural Similarity Analysis. *Proceedings of IEEE Workshop on* was expected that there would either be no difference between groups, as found by previous studies, or that FT participants might perform better at the task. Instead the study found the exact opposite. IT participants showed more consensus in both aspects of the experiment, and were more likely to choose the structural boundary identified by score analysis than their FT counterparts. These findings would support those of Bigand & Poulin-Charronnat (2006), that one does not need formal training to become an 'experienced listener'.

Questions remain, however, as to why the variation between participant groups was so pronounced. Further research would need to use a larger and wider sample in order to fully account for this. There is the possibility that the variation is due to some identified methodological limitations. The version of musicological analysis employed in this study was necessarily limited in order to define a simple method of equating musicological and computational analysis. The selection of only five features, four defined and one undefined, would inevitably impact on the level of analysis possible. The term *structural boundary* was replaced with *most significant point of feature change* in the instructions to participants, on the assumption that the two were commensurate, in line with the reasoning of Addessi & Caterina (2002). This was not always the case, as exemplified by the results of Excerpt 2, where no participants perceived a boundary at either point generated by the analysis methods. Further research is required to test the robustness of these approaches in evaluating other pieces of music.

Finally, it was necessary to use computational feature extraction in order to acquire temporal points that reaction windows could be linked to. This proved problematic since the computational system used relied heavily on single feature analysis, and human perception (and musicological analysis) does not. The series of functions used provided the nearest approximation, in our estimation, to a perceptual approach, basing computations on analysis of a spectrogram which could account for a wider range of features, particularly when time-decomposed. The limitation of such a system was that, as identified by Leman et al. (2005), the extracted points still needed to be related to musical features using musicological analysis. Also, as was evident in the differences between the MSP, the PGN, and the relative number of responses linked to each, our findings further supported those of Leman at al. in that 'manual structural cues worked better than acoustical structural cues.' (Leman et al. 2005, 59).

Applications of Signal Processing to Audio and Acoustics (WASPAA), 127-130.

Irene Deliège, 1987. Grouping Conditions in Listening to Music: An Approach to Lerdahl & Jackendoff's Grouping Preference Rules. *Music Perception*, Vol. 4, No. 4, 325-360.

Irene Deliège & Abessadek El Ahnmadi, 1990. Mechanisms of Cue Extraction in Musical Groupings: A Study of Perception on Sequenza VI for Viola Solo by Luciano Berio. *Psychology of Music*, 18, 18-44.

Jonathan Foote, 1999. Visualising Music and Audio Using Self-Similarity. *Proceedings of ACM Multimedia '99*. Orlando, FL: ACM Press, 77-80.

Carolyn Granier-Deferre & Marie-Claire Busnel, 2013. Human Fetal Auditory Perception. Fetal Development: A Psychobiological Perspective, 239.

Carol L. Krumhansl, 1996. A perceptual analysis of Mozart's Piano Sonata K. 282: Segmentation, tension, and musical ideas. *Music Perception*, 13, 401-432.

Marc Leman, Valerie Vermeulen, Liesbeth De Voogdt, Dirk Moelants & Micheline Lesaffre, 2005. Prediction of musical affect using a combination of acoustic structural cues. *Journal of New Music Research*, 34(1), 39-67.

Fred Lerdahl & Ray Jackendoff, 1983. *A Generative Theory of Tonal Music*. Cambridge, Mass.: MIT Press.

Adam Ockelford, 2005. *Repetition in Music: Theoretical and Metatheoretical Perspectives*. Aldershot: Ashgate Pub. Ltd.

Naphtali Wagner, 1995. No Crossing Branches? The Overlapping Technique in Schenkerian Analysis. *Theory and Practice*, Vol. 20, 149-175.